ACCLAIM

BranchCreek Community Church is uniquely effective in their local outreach, hospitality ministries, and dynamic worship services. And the church is blessed with one of the nation's top communicators in Craig Bishop. Craig's ability to disclose a practical spirituality through speaking and writing has a deep impact on the lives of thousands of people at his church and beyond. BranchCreek has used studies such as this for a congregation-wide fall spiritual emphasis for the past five years, resulting in great growth. It looks like this one will be another winner. I highly commend this important message to the body of Christ at large.

> Kevin G. Ford, author of *Transforming Church* and Managing Partner of TAG, Fairfax, Virginia

Artfully crafted and engaging, Craig Bishop's *Discovering Your Divine Design* will gently push you to explore and live out your unique contribution to God's Kingdom. Beware! If you follow this road map, it just may revolutionize your life of service!

> Andrew Accardy, Canterbury Partners (Former Executive Vice President, Purpose Driven)
> Atlanta, Georgia

The wisdom and knowledge I found in this work by Craig Bishop puts forth a road map for a rich and fulfilling life, one which will please God and His followers. It is amazing to me the amount of living, study and discipline that went into this book. I certainly recommend this to anyone.

> Michael Smyser, B.F.A., M.F.A., Professor Emeritus of Fine Arts
> Montgomery County Community College
> Blue Bell, Pennsylvania

Discovering Your Divine Design not only guides readers into understanding their own unique God-designed makeup, but motivates them to use their unique design to advance the Kingdom. With inspired biblical insight, Dr. Bishop gives practical how-to's in discovering, clarifying and growing in the use of our spiritual gifts. He uses wonderful personal anecdotes to demonstrate the process. And he makes it clear that it is a lifetime process. The questions in the "Reflection" section at the end of each chapter are thought provoking and suitable for either individual use or group discussions. I believe readers will be motivated and encouraged to move ahead in becoming all God has designed them to be.

> Jimmy Lee, President, Living Free Ministries
> Chattanooga, Tennessee

Craig is a great pastor, leader and friend, and this all comes through in his writing. Some works about God's design in each of us can raise more questions than they answer – not this one. It feels like an "across the back fence" chat with a guy who knows a bunch and cares even more. These chapters are thoughtfully written and easily understood and I know will be encouraging to many!

Greg Gibbs, Vice President, Cargill Associates
Fort Worth, Texas

I believe in Craig and his heart for the church. Helping people discover their unique design for ministry and mobilizing them to make an impact is his clear passion and a vital need for today's church. This book creatively takes readers through the essential components to identify their calling as Christ followers. I am confident that those who read it will be further equipped, challenged and motivated to walk God's path for them. Read it, apply it, live it – and you and those around you will be blessed!

Mike Harder, Sonlife Ministries East Coast Director
Youth and Young Adults Pastor, BranchCreek Community Church,
Harleysville, Pennsylvania

Craig Bishop has written a terrific detailed and practical guide to self-discovery in his book *Discovering Your Divine Design*. Craig is a practitioner of life, not just a theorist, and it shows in this book. I strongly endorse this book, which is the product of decades dealing with the topic and its application.

Doug Murren, Square One Ministries
Author of *Leader Shift, Baby Boomerang* and *Keeping Your Dreams Alive*
Boise, Idaho

Anchored in scriptural truth throughout, *Discovering Your Divine Design* is an insightful and practical guide to finding exciting purpose and godly direction in your life. This book is a powerful tool for putting your gifts to work to impact the Kingdom.

Dan Chaverin
Pittsburg, Pennsylvania

Every human being is unique and special. Every follower couples this divine wiring with a divine calling and mission. Dr. Craig Bishop's book, *Discovering Your Divine Design*, provides both insightful teaching regarding our SHAPE as well as reflection exercises to help us further discover, develop and utilize our capabilities. As you read this book and apply its teaching to your life, you will become all that God intends.

Dr. Glenn E. Pfeiffer – Pastor of LifePoint Church
Harrisburg, Pennsylvania

DISCOVERING YOUR
DiViNE DESiGN

*a 50-day devotional to help you
understand your uniqueness*

dr. s. craig bishop

Discovering Your Divine Design

A 50-Day Devotional to Help You Understand Your Uniqueness

Dr. S. Craig Bishop

Requests for information should be addressed to:
Dr. S. Craig Bishop
BranchCreek Community Church
100 South Main Street
Harleysville, Pennsylvania 19438

ISDN #978-0-9761772-2-7
1. Christian Living

For Bible translations used, see Appendix 1

Quantity sales and special discounts are available on quantity purchases by churches and Christian organizations. Requests for information should be addressed to BranchCreek Community Church, 100 South Main Street, Harleysville, Pennsylvania 19438.

Cover photo by Ioseph
Cover design by Michael Allebach
Interior design by Michael Allebach

Printed in the USA

Contents

Acknowledgments and Dedication.................................. 9

Preface 11

1. Drawing Back the Curtain 13
2. Starting on the Journey 17
3. Following Your Guide 21
4. Avoiding Distractions 25
5. Reviving the Dream 29
6. Your Unique Shape 33
7. Understanding Spiritual Gifts 37
8. Putting Spiritual Gifts to Work 43
9. Understanding Heart 47
10. Putting Your Heart to Work 51
11. Understanding Abilities 55
12. Putting Your Abilities to Work 59
13. Understanding Personality 63
14. Putting Your Personality to Work 69
15. Understanding Experiences 73
16. Putting Your Experiences to Work 77
17. Take Inventory 81
18. Now Put It All Together 85
19. Potholes and Roadblocks 89
20. Me, Myself and Why 93
21. Your Divine Design and God's Will 97
22. Extreme Makeovers of the Mind 101
23. The Importance of Pause, Prayer and Reflection 105
24. The Values Matrix 109
25. Your Sweet Spot 113
26. Your Statement of Mission 117
27. It's All About Service 121
28. Ready to Risk It? 125
29. Faith to Implement 129
30. Finding the Spark 133
31. Fanning the Flame 137
32. A Raging Fire 141

33. Sustaining the Gains 145

34. Doubts, Defeats and Discouragements 149

35. Life's Priorities and Choices 153

36. Life Seasons 157

37. The Master Requires Mastery............................... 161

38. Family Implications 165

39. Implications for Your Work 169

40. Income-ing 173

41. The Danger of Burnout 177

42. Seeing Life Differently 181

43. Opening the Door to Others 185

44. The Next Step.............................. 189

45. Character Matters........................... 193

46. Tracking the Design to the Designer........................ 197

47. Complete Surrender...................... 201

48. The Role of the Local Church 205

49. A Kingdom Force 209

50. A New Life Story 213

Conclusion.................... 217

A Word to Pastors................. 219

Endnotes 222

Resources 229

Appendix 1: Translations.................. 230

Appendix 2: Contact Information 232

ACKNOWLEDGMENTS
AND DEDICATION

An author should never conceive himself as bringing into existence beauty or wisdom which did not exist before, but simply and solely as trying to embody in terms of his own arts some reflection of eternal beauty and wisdom.
— C. S. Lewis

Discovering Your Divine Design was inspired by over 3,500 BranchCreek Community Church attenders, who through their dedication and commitment, have made the 32-year ride of this pastor way beyond exciting.

It has been their passion for God's ways and God's Word that has kept me so motivated to explore our Kingdom potential.

Thank you, my friends, for your examples of love, acceptance and service that extend from the first-time guest to those who have been here since the beginning.

I also must acknowledge the superlative management skills of chuck faber, my close associate and dear friend, who overloaded his schedule so that I could free mine to find the necessary time for writing.

I wish to thank my children, Matthew, Angela and Charity, for enduring our mutual explorations surrounding their career paths and my first feeble attempts to explain to them my understanding of their Divine Design. Thanks too for your graciousness during my emotional roller coaster ride as writing deadlines would approach.

Special thanks to my four-year-old granddaughter Alexa who gave up some of our precious playtime so "Pop-Pop could teach big people how to have fun too."

And most of all, I wish to express my deepest gratitude to my dear wife of 32 years, Sally. No book I've ever written could have surfaced from my soul without you — and least of all this one. Your tireless efforts in typing the manuscript, your creative insights, your amazing attention to detail have made your Divine Design one that I will cherish spending my life studying. Thank you for using your gifts to help people use theirs. I wish to dedicate this book to you.

Last of all I wish to acknowledge all my readers who have the curiosity and spiritual courage to seek out their Divine Design and act on it!

Realizing it takes a team to accomplish anything significant, I wish to thank our ministry workers at BranchCreek Community Church who helped in the creative research, typing, editing, proofing, formatting, production and promotion of Discovering Your Divine Design so that it would be ready for your consideration. Each one understood and utilized his or her own design and offered it in service to help me complete this task to God's glory.

S. Craig Bishop, D. Min.
Harleysville, Pennsylvania
September 2007

PREFACE

Moreover, human life would seem to consist in that in which each man most delights, that for which he especially strives, and that which he particularly wishes to share with his friends...

— St. Thomas Aquinas

You may not be aware of the fact that you are a unique expression of a creative God. He fashioned you to fulfill His purpose while you are on earth. You have been preprogrammed with an unmatched combination of desires, drives, capabilities and orientation toward life that allows you to walk this earth in a way unlike any other. You have a Divine Design! This book is written to help you through the maze of your personal discovery process. But once you have made your discoveries, you must commit yourself to develop the habits necessary to utilize the gifts you've been given.

The research for this book has led me to several conclusions, which I present as assumptions. The first is, everyone is gifted. There are some capabilities that you have that, when practiced, are unlike those of any 100,000 other people. Secondly, your Divine Design is unique. Just like there are no two flowers or snowflakes or birds exactly alike, there are no two people alike either. In fact, you are dissimilar to anyone who has ever visited the planet or ever will. Thirdly, your specific pattern of giftedness has been functioning since birth and will continue to guide you until you die. As long as you are breathing you cannot escape it. In fact, there are good indications from the Bible that your heavenly experience may be an extension of your earthly one and that you will continue to utilize your design for eternity. Everything about your design was God's idea.

In this volume, I talk primarily about those things that we consider gifts or strengths. There are parts of ourselves about which we have doubts and apprehensions – areas that we are not excited about or proud of. We must remember that these are part of our humanity and to understand them is in fact a gift to our growth and maturity because the things that we cannot do contribute just as much to our understanding of our Devine Design as those that we can do. Our limitations point to our finiteness, and being in touch with our own limitations helps us to accept the limitations of others. Our limitations also help to make us more dependent on God.

This was Paul's point in Romans 12:4-6 when he pointed out that it takes all of us to make the body complete. If we labor under the delusion that we can do it all, we are unlikely to turn to our Creator.

God said in Isaiah 46:10 (NIV), "I make known the end from the beginning, from ancient times, what is still to come. I say: My purpose will stand, and I will do all that I please."

- God has created you to fulfill His purpose for your life
- Everything you do is affected by your Divine Design. Not only what you do but how you do it, and why you do it.
- His Divine Design is your essence. It's a treasure that needs to be discovered, developed and deployed so that your journey on earth has maximum fulfillment and fruitfulness.
- God requires you to love Him and those you serve with passion and excellence
- God will hold you accountable for the use of your Divine Design
- God will increase your effectiveness as you use your Divine Design
- God wants you to help expand His Kingdom using your Divine Design

So let's get started. Your journey will have many personal rewards and rich benefits for God, for you, and for others.

CHAPTER 1

DRAWING BACK THE CURTAIN

It's not a place you can get to by a boat or train . . .
– Dorothy in the Wizard of Oz

It seems all of us are born with an innate desire to arrive in a land in which all our questions about life will be answered. Much like Dorothy setting off on the yellow brick road in Frank Baum's classic Wizard of Oz, we assume that if we follow the proper path we will soon arrive at an emerald city that contains all the resources we will need to get us to our ultimate destination.

Of course the questions most perplexing are those that have to do with ourselves.

- Why do I like certain things and dislike others?
- Why do I love certain people and detest others?
- Why do some tasks generate such excitement I can't wait to do them, while I put off others?

And these questions are just a subset of others that are more difficult and profound.

- Why am I here?
- What is the purpose for my existence?
- What am I supposed to be doing?
- Are there goals and values that transcend my brief life?
- Were my past experiences random, or do they have a specific meaning?

The Dorothy in all of us would like to draw back the curtain of the famous wizard to see if there is anyone at the controls and, if so, to determine when and why the levers in our life are about to be moved.

Well, congratulations. At least you've had the clarity of thinking to realize you're not in Kansas anymore! You've started a journey. And whether you realize it or not, your effort will be rewarded. Yes, there are answers to the questions you ask.

I suspect you know that already. The unrest in your heart points to the truth that you were designed by a Designer . . . created for creativity. As Abraham Maslow states, "If you deliberately set out to be less than you are capable, you'll be unhappy for the rest of your life." And so you press on. Uncertain of the outcome, you continue the search because your eyes look for opportunity. You continue reading this page because your ears listen for direction and your mind longs for a challenge. And whether you realize it or not, your heart craves truth.

In other words, YOU WERE MADE FOR MORE! They've done some interesting studies on this. (One day I'm going to find out who "they" are, because they do some great studies.) After looking at 2 million people, they've discovered each of us can do one or two or three things better than any other 100,000 people![1]

That means the Creator of the universe has made an investment in you and you need to realize He's expecting a return. No doubt you have figured out by now that every moment you waste not pursuing your purpose is a missed opportunity. You probably know that the goals of prosperity, popularity and power are ultimately unfulfilling. Contrary to what others try to tell you, they aren't the big ideas for life. They don't clear up life's fog; they contribute to it.

Are you tired of stumbling halfheartedly through life hoping for a better tomorrow? Do you fear that as you turn the pages of your life story, the final chapter is approaching and there's been no significant plot development? The story will certainly take you somewhere . . . but by purpose or by accident?

Here is some great news. Everyone can have a meaningful and fulfilling life. It isn't the result of luck, background, education or influential friends. You don't have to possess extraordinary talent or be born in the right neighborhood. All you have to do is make a commitment to discover your Divine Design.

The book that serves as a road map for that journey is the Bible. In its pages you will discover that you were created for a unique reason. In other words, God has a dream for you – a big idea. A personal mission. It is a consequence of our being fashioned like Him. The first book of the Bible tells us that we were made in His image, and if God is anything, He is a

God of purpose.[2] Max Lucado says, "If God can speak from a burning bush to a shepherd called Moses, then he can speak from a mop bucket to a janitor called Hank."[3] God has given every one of us a special area of expertise. We weren't stamped out on an assembly line or mass-produced to be like everyone else. The Bible makes it clear that each created being is a custom design, a one-of-a-kind, original masterpiece.

But the big question is "created for what?" We know from observing our surroundings that form must follow function. In other words, when God made us He decided the role that He wanted each of us to play. He then included the necessary gifts, talents, passion and personality in our design. We are the way we are for a reason. Consider these words from Psalm 139:

> . . . You created my inmost being;
> You knit me together in my mother's womb.
> I praise you because I am fearfully and wonderfully made;
> Your works are wonderful,
> I know that full well.
> My frame was not hidden from You
> When I was made in the secret place.
> When I was woven together in the depths of the earth,
> Your eyes saw my unformed body.
> All the days ordained for me
> Were written in Your book
> Before one of them came to be.[4]

You stand alone among billions. You are the culmination of a divine plan. Being pressured to conform, tempted to compare, enticed to compete, baited into compromise – these will corrupt and spoil your design. You were made for a mission! God expects you to discover, develop and deploy your uniqueness so that you can live out His perfect plan for your life. As you do, you will fulfill His and your greatest hopes and dreams. Be bold! Have the courage to pull back the curtain of life, and when you do, you'll discover that there really is someone at the controls.

REFLECTION

1. When in your life did you first think that you were made for more? How did you react to that feeling?
2. Can you give an example of a time when the outcome of your efforts was surprisingly poor? How about when the result was so much more than you were expecting? Can you identify the reasons for this?
3. Why is it unlikely that you will discover your Divine Design until you pursue it?
4. Why can we be sure God's dream for us is worthy of our pursuit?
5. Read John 10:10. Explain why the stealing of a Divine destiny may be life's greatest tragedy.

CHAPTER 2

STARTING ON THE JOURNEY

I had been my whole life a bell, and never knew it until at that moment I was lifted and struck.
    — Annie Dillard

Cathy and 8,500 other patients of a local hospital received their bills, along with some shocking news: They had died! Apparently a computer glitch was responsible. Cathy said, "I was pretty sure I was not dead, but you never know."[1]

Are you living a fulfilling life? Or are you a dead man (or woman) walking? Do the roles you pursue and the work you do fill your heart with passion? Or are you so busy cutting through the undergrowth that you don't even realize you are in the wrong jungle?

Do you live with an ongoing sense of purpose and meaning? You may be surprised to discover that the majority of people would answer "No!" to that question. A staggering number of people float down the river of life with no anchor, no oars and no sail. Occasionally, and often coincidentally, they drift into a port but have no means to fasten themselves to the dock.

Life can be better when you discover your niche. William Ellery Channing stated, "Every human is intended to have a character of his own, to be what no others are and to do what no others can do." God designed a vessel for you to navigate, a map for you to follow and a song for you to sing along the way.

More than a thousand references in the Old and New Testaments tell us that God has a plan for our lives and we are to follow it. Consider Colossians 1:16 (MES), which states, "For everything, absolutely everything, above and below, visible and invisible . . . everything got started in Him and finds its purpose in Him." The intended outcome of this journey of ours pushes the limits of imagination. As Keith Miller and Bruce Larson put it,

> All that we are meant to be! God's dream for each of us is so vastly greater than the largest dream we have for ourselves. But what is His dream for us? I believe He has given us clues to what that dream is. And the longings and yearnings buried in each of us often provide those clues. It is like being on a cosmic treasure

hunt. Follow one clue and it will lead you to another . . . and then to another . . . and then to another . . . until you find the treasure Himself. For to find God and His ultimate will for us is to find ourselves. This is the discovery for which all creation stands on tiptoe – to see God's sons and daughters coming into their own.[2]

The starting point of our journey is much more than just an inner exploration. Many make the mistake of assuming that life's journey is a hunting expedition to find themselves. But like searching for the elusive "bigfoot," we may see prints that resemble ours, shadows in the bushes, a blur in the distance, yet our bigfoot catch remains just out of reach.

I know the introspective search to find "me" was fruitless. A pipe-smoking philosophy professor directed my college class to begin journaling an evaluation of life and our role in the world. "Why were we here and what did we expect to contribute?" he asked. Now decades later as I review those notes I laugh at my conclusions. After months of navel-gazing I ended my journey exactly where I started – unsure and confused.

I've since discovered that solutions to life's challenges require a good beginning. The viewpoint is very important. Whether you start inside or outside yourself makes a big difference. A person with his or her head inside a paper bag will have a much different personal viewpoint than a person whose head is outside of it.

Each of us is stuck inside a body within a region of territory, a part of a huge but definable land mass inside the atmosphere of a planet that is within a particular galaxy. To understand our role in human history we need the viewpoint of the Creator of the cosmos, not the oxygen-deprived impressions of a nearly asphyxiated being blinking in the darkness of a paper bag.

And the only way we can know the truth about our Creator is for Him to communicate it to us. He has made the truth of the universe known through the pages of the Bible. And if there is one thing we can be certain of, it's that each of us has value to Him.

The Bible puts it this way:

> "For we are God's masterpiece. He has created us anew in Christ Jesus, so that we can do the good things He planned for us long ago." Ephesians 2:10 (NLT)

In other words, each of us is a unique work of divine art. There is no one else like you, and your Heavenly Father longs for you to discover your special place in the world. After all, God makes everything special – not only people, but flowers, trees, animals, snowflakes.

If you try to live without discovering your uniqueness, you will miss God's divine plan and your unique purpose. Don't risk it!

Consider what Max Lucado says in his book *Cure for the Common Life:*

> Da Vinci painted one Mona Lisa, Beethoven created one 5th Symphony, and God made one version of you. You're it! You're the only you there is. And if we don't get you, we don't get you. You are the only shot we have at you. You can do something no one else can do in a fashion no one else can do it. You are more than a coincidence of chromosomes and heredity, more than just an assemblage of somebody else's lineage. You are uniquely made . . . [3]

As I write these words there's a bit of turmoil going on in the art community over a recently discovered Jackson Pollack painting. While Pollack's creations often fetch millions of dollars, the latest one turned up in a secondhand shop and was sold to an elderly female truck driver for $8. The painting clearly matches his earlier works, and a fingerprint on the back of the canvas has been matched to a print from one of his paint cans. In a snobbish attempt to vilify its owner, the art community refuses to acknowledge the newly discovered painting as genuine.

How very often we are like that community of artists. Using arbitrary and unproven evaluation techniques, we look at ourselves and don't see the value. We don't see God's brush strokes on the canvas, nor His fingerprint on the design. Meanwhile, we rush to another work of the same artist, all gaga and goggle-eyed at what we think is a far better rendering than the one we have.

When God made you, He made no mistakes. You are special. Psalm 139:15 (MES) states that you have been "sculpted from nothing into something." It isn't that we need more strength, greater ability or new opportunities. We simply need to accept and use what we have been given. If God is the masterpiece painter, then we can be sure that His canvas is big. Just like any art critic, what you see is going to depend a great deal on what you look for. J. Oswald Sanders says that "Eyes that look are common. Eyes that see are rare."

Here is what God wants you to see: " 'For I know the plans I have for you,' declares the Lord. 'Plans to prosper you and not to harm you, plans to give you a hope and a future.' " Jeremiah 29:11 (TLB)

You are about to view one of God's most complex and astounding creations – you!

REFLECTION

1. What do you do best?
2. What do you enjoy doing?
3. Why do you think most people ignore their responses to the questions above and are content to "drift" through life?
4. If each of us is unique, why are we so likely to pursue others' expectations of us?
5. Read Romans 12:5-9. Give an example of a time when you ignored the truth of these verses. How did things turn out?

CHAPTER 3

FOLLOWING YOUR GUIDE

Mediocrity is a region bounded on the north by compromise, on the south by indecision, on the east by past thinking, and on the west by a lack of vision.
— John L. Mason

All the maps in the world won't get you to a destination if you don't pull them out and look at them. The best guide in the country can't get you to a location unless you decide to follow him. But the journey is not always easy.

Jack London's books are epic stories of men and women on their way to the Yukon gold fields. If they chose the water route along the coast of Alaska and then upriver, they had to brave the storms of the Bering Sea. The ice in the Yukon River could rip their boats to shreds. If they took the overland trail, they faced miles of mud and snow over almost impenetrable mountains. Many died just attempting to get to the boomtowns. Once there, they had to brave long days of backbreaking labor and long nights cramped in lean-to cabins with their companions. Injury in those isolated places often meant death. Still, they came by the thousands. The journey was dangerous and the work was difficult, but to those men and women gold was worth the risk.

Is our hope any less than theirs? Is our prize any less valuable? After all, their path was temporal; ours is eternal. They did, however, have one distinct advantage over us – they could see, hold and touch their treasure. Our treasure is unseen. We need to ask God to open our eyes to see the reality of our spiritual claim. Then we, like the Yukon miners, will gladly endure every hardship and any sacrifice to obtain it.

Here is a statement to take along. In Ephesians 1:4 (NIV), Paul says, "For He chose us before the creation of the world . . ."

In other words, no matter what you think about yourself and no matter what someone else tells you, you have a Divine Design and destiny. You've been handcrafted for a specific purpose, chosen to live at precisely this time to accomplish a purpose that is yours alone. In other words, you have been made "you"-nique. One famous philosopher expressed it like this:

> At each man's birth there comes into being an eternal vocation
> for him, expressly for him. To be true to himself in relation to
> this eternal vocation is the highest thing a man can practice.[1]

I will always love the enduring song "The Impossible Dream." It was a part of my high school district chorus presentation. We had to learn all the music from the Broadway play, *Man of La Mancha*. Perhaps you are familiar with the story. It tells the tale of a medieval knight who meets a woman of the street, a prostitute. But this poet-knight sees something else in her, something beautiful and lovely. He sees her virtue, and he affirms it, over and over again. He gives her a new name – Dulcinea. She resists her new identity and writes the man off as a wild-eyed fantasizer. But he is persistent. He makes continual deposits of unconditional love and it goes down into her true nature, her potential, and she starts to respond. And little by little she changes her lifestyle. When she has a relapse he calls her to his deathbed, looks into her eyes, sings that beautiful song, "The Impossible Dream," and whispers, "Never forget, you are Dulcinea."

God does the same with us. He takes you where you are but makes you more than you are. His unconditional love and complete acceptance can cause a complete transformation for you. Ezra Taft Benson states: "The Lord works from the inside out. The world works from the outside in. The world would take people out of the slums. Christ takes the slums out of people, and then they take themselves out of the slums. The world would mold men by changing their environment. Christ changes men, who then change their environment. The world would shape human behavior, but Christ can change human nature."

When God sets you on your life journey, He doesn't pack you up on a cruise ship along with thousands of others heading to the exact same place. No, your tour of life is one of a kind – carefully planned and including all the luggage and necessities you'll need for maximum excitement and enjoyment. You will notice that your suitcases have your name on them. As you begin to unpack the gifts, personality, passion and experiences that are a part of your unique belongings, you will be surprised at God's thoughtfulness. You may discover some unexpected things inside, but don't worry – they were packed with love and care, and at the appropriate time you will find that you need them.

Traveling to Phoenix, I arrived at my hotel to prepare for a conference I was attending. Imagine my surprise as I flipped open my suitcase to get a change of clothes and out popped a shimmering blue sequined dress. Somehow between the Philadelphia airport and my Phoenix hotel, I had mistakenly traded suitcases with one lady who was surely, by now, very disappointed with my idea of evening attire. A quick rush to the store made me late for the event, but this was preferable to demonstrating my skills in cross-dressing to a thousand pastors.

When God packs your bags, He never gets them mixed up. You have been designed to make a one-of-a-kind fashion statement. Your apparel is custom-tailored and completely appropriate for life's upcoming events. By seeing what's been packed *in* we understand more of what we're to work out. Paul puts it this way in Galatians 6:4 (MES):

> ". . . make a careful exploration of who you are and the work you have been given and then sink yourself into that."

If you really want to make a difference in the world, then you have to learn to accept your true identity. Don't follow the crowd. Don't wear someone else's clothes. As Herman Melville wrote, "It is better to fail in originality than to succeed in imitation."

Conformity will squash your joy and limit your growth. Don't be afraid to be different because God made you with a difference. After all, who's better qualified to be you than you? One of the main purposes of your life is to allow the true "you" to emerge. But in American society, there are many other voices.

You have to decide which voice you're going to listen to – the voice of others, the voice inside your head or God's voice. The Bible states in Genesis 1:31 (NRS) that "God saw everything that He made and, indeed, it was very good."

In other words, even before you hit the planet running (or crawling, I should say), God saw you as you would be. You have already received His approval and were delivered right on time. He knew the specific purpose you were designed to fulfill and He provided you the gifts you'd need, the personality to pull it off, the passion to inspire you, and the environment that would bring it all together. Then he looked at you and said, "Very good! This will do it."

Can you say that too? I hope so, because that's where our guide on this journey of life is leading us. And there is no way you are going to get to your intended destination without following your guide.

REFLECTION

1. Give an example of a time when you were sure God was guiding you in the use of your unique abilities. What was the outcome? How did you feel?

2. If God chose you before the creation of the world, why do you think He elected this place and time to introduce your gifts and skills to the planet?

3. If God has a very specific purpose for us to accomplish, why do you think it is so difficult for so many to discover it?

4. What steps are you feeling God wants you to take to help in your understanding of His design?

5. Read Philippians 3:13-14. Paraphrase this verse in your own words in a way that gives direction for your next week.

CHAPTER 4

AVOIDING DISTRACTIONS

. . . God has already revealed His will to us concerning our vocation and Mission, by causing it to be "written in our members." We are to begin deciphering our unique Mission by studying our talents and skills, and more particularly which ones (or one) we most rejoice to use.
– Richard N. Bolles

Those who follow the self-help gurus who advocate the benefits of positive thinking or PMA (positive mental attitude) often make statements such as "If it's to be it's up to me" or "You can be anything you want to be." The idea is that if you work hard enough at something you can achieve it.

There are several problems with this concept. The first is, it has its limitations. For example, do you think that if you worked hard enough you could become a rocket scientist or a concert pianist or a neurosurgeon? Well, you couldn't be a rocket scientist if you aren't good with numbers. And you couldn't be a concert pianist if your hands can't stretch far enough for the chords required in some of the great concertos. And you couldn't be a neurosurgeon if you have trouble memorizing the parts of the body. Even apart from the skills involved, one or more of these vocations may not even interest you. You may have no desire to do them. And how far could you get in their pursuit without desire? A poorly suited role is like a poorly fitted piece of clothing. It can seem obvious to everyone but the wearer.

No, God didn't put you on earth to find a place but to find *your* place. Søren Kierkegaard stated, "What I lack is to be clear in my mind what I am to do, not what I am to know . . . the thing is to understand myself, to see what God really wishes me to do . . . to find the idea for which I can live and die."[1]

We're not going to hit the bull's-eye if we're shooting at the wrong target. But it's easy to get pulled aside and distracted by the good and fail to pursue the best. And who could blame us? First of all, our society shines the spotlight on certain gifts and abilities that seem to get all the glory. Sing well enough to fill auditoriums, be athletic enough to fill stadiums or be attractive and artistic enough to command movie roles and your life will be littered with accolades. It seems we have a certain cultural bias toward success because lesser-known abilities are very often not even recognized as abilities. For example, when's the last time you heard someone being honored for an ability to read instruction manuals? Who do you know who's ever received recognition for pulling weeds at a public park? Where do they give out awards for people who enjoy fixing broken toys or appliances?

Because our society looks at success through a certain lens, many of us may go through life feeling as though we don't deserve to have our picture taken. We ignore our Divine Design and focus on success as our society measures it. This often distracts us from our true purpose.

We also minimize our own gifts and abilities because our focus is outward. We tend to recognize gifts in others more readily than we see them in ourselves. Because certain abilities come easy to us, we don't recognize them as special. We assume everyone can do the same things we can, just as easily.

Sometimes when we are complimented for a certain skill we will minimize it with statements such as "Aw, it was nuthin' " or "No big deal." But little things to us may be a very big deal to others. For example, suppose this manuscript was filled with grammatical and typographical errors. (I hope not!) It may surprise those of you who spot these kinds of things to know that some people are absolutely blind to them. Almost a dozen eyes will review this page for errors, yet I can promise you that some day, when this manuscript is far from my mind, I will receive an e-mail from someone who will point out an error. And what a great service they provide!

Romans 12:6 (NLT) expresses it this way: "God has given each of us the ability to do certain things well."

What comes easily to you may be extremely difficult to your neighbor. While you can't do everything, you can do something that no one else can do in a way that no one else can do it.

Remember the story of Charlie Steinmetz? He designed the huge generators that were the power source for Henry Ford's assembly lines in Deerborne, Michigan. Soon after he retired, so did the generators, bringing the entire plant to a halt. After Ford's engineers gave up, Henry called his old friend Charlie. Eyewitnesses said that Charlie fiddled with this gauge, jiggled a lever, pushed a couple buttons, played with a few wires, tapped on some transformers. After a couple hours of this seemingly crazy behavior, Charlie threw the master switch. The motors kicked on, causing a smile on Charlie's face. Days later Ford received a bill from Charlie for $10,000. Never one to spend a nickel more than he had to, Henry wrote his friend a note: "Charlie, it seems awful steep, this $10,000, for a man who for just a little while tinkered around with a few motors." Charlie wrote a new itemized bill and sent it back to Mr. Ford.

> Henry,
>
> For tinkering around with the motors $ 10
> For knowing where to tinker $ 9,990
> Total $10,000[2]

You can't do anything you want to do, but you can do some things that nearly no one else can do. You tinker unlike anyone else. Discover and develop your tinkering talent until you become expert in it. The reward for your effort will be far more than financial. Ephesians 6:8 (NCV) states: "Remember that the Lord will give a reward to everyone . . . for doing good."

I once played a joke on my sister at a shoreside shooting gallery. After she was reluctantly coaxed into playing the game, I watched her carefully line up her first shot. I was standing slightly behind her, holding an electronic pistol of my own. Since she had no experience, I was relatively certain she would miss her shot. I aimed my own gun and squeezed the silent trigger just as she released hers. Only I aimed at a different target. When a tin can shot up in the air instead of the clang of a cow bell, everyone laughed.

Impressed that she made something move, Sherry aimed at her next target (as did I). By now the more experienced shooters in our group had caught on. But my sister was deeply engrossed and mildly encouraged by her newfound skill. As long as something happened, she didn't much care what it moved.

As a life analogy, both of us were off base. Sherry was motivated by movement, not efficiency. I was taking a good shot but hitting the wrong target. Both are common on the journey toward our Divine Design. And both are distractions. You can fail to develop your gifts and abilities because you're too easily satisfied, distracted by the puff of smoke surrounding your recently relocated tin can. After all, something moved. Or, you can become extremely good at improving your efficiency while taking aim at the wrong target.

We must stay focused. Paul wrote in I Corinthians 10:23 (NIV), "All things are lawful for me, but not all things are helpful." Some things are not necessarily wrong, but they're just not necessary. They waste time and distract you. They may belong on someone else's agenda but not yours.

Successful people stay focused on the truly important: To make strides toward understanding your Divine Design, avoid distractions.

REFLECTION

1. Describe a poorly suited role in which you served. How did it make you feel? What effect did it have on others? How did it change you and how did you change it?
2. Why is it fruitless to try to imitate the success someone else has achieved in an area?
3. What were the results you experienced when you tried to do something for which you had no talent or ability? Can you give an example?
4. Have you ever tried taking a shortcut to a "successful" life? What did you do and how did it turn out?
5. Matthew 5:48 (MES) states, "In a word, what I'm saying is, grow up. You're Kingdom subjects. Now live like it. Live out your God-created identity." If Jesus had written this to you personally, what life situation of yours might He be describing?

CHAPTER 5

REVIVING THE DREAM

The past is prologue.

— A sign in front of the National Archives,
Washington, D.C.

Imagine your life as a movie. If you are in your 20s you've arrived in time to see previews of coming attractions. If you are in your 30s you've arrived at the film after it began. You may be missing a bit of the setting and the context of the motion picture. If you are in your 40s the film has reached its midpoint. You can only guess at what you might have missed. If you are in your 50s the movie has established most of its plot points and set up tension that waits for resolution. If you are in your 60s (or older) the film nears its conclusion but you have yet to see the climax and how the unresolved issues will be addressed. But, no matter where you are in life's motion picture, there are still things you don't know or yet understand. There are still lessons to be learned. It's never too late to set your imagination loose and dream about the possibilities.

You were created for a purpose, and God needs you to do something on earth that no one else can do. He designed you to do it better than anyone else could. It may relate to the way you make people feel at ease, the sense of humor you have, the way you build a business, how you design or decorate, your ability to tell stories or your capacity to see the crux of a problem. When you do what God has given you to do in the way that He has made you to do it, He is delighted. Not only is He pleased, but He uses your efforts to accomplish His grand scheme for the ages.

When I was in elementary school I had a dream. It was to play in the school band. Each student had his or her own instrument, and I desperately wanted to play. My problem was that my parents didn't have the money to buy me an instrument, much less give me lessons. I asked the band director if there was any instrument that no one else wanted to play. He informed me that there was one. It was called a sousaphone – a large, belching instrument much like a tuba. He said he had just ordered one for the orchestra and as soon as it came in he would teach me to play it. I was thrilled. Every Friday afternoon for the next 17 weeks I headed down to the band room to ask the director if my cherished polished piece of metal had arrived. I spent every night before bed imagining myself playing this impressive instrument and wowing my fellow band members with its melodies. Of course I had no idea what a sousaphone sounded like – I had just learned to say the word.

Finally, my cherished melody maker arrived. I was most surprised that it had only three keys. My band leader assured me I would be able to play more than three notes. As I practiced, I found it curious that I made sounds with this big instrument by essentially spitting into the mouthpiece. The kids laughed at little me and my monstrosity, but I didn't care. I exalted in the bursts and burps of sound made by passing air through the circular brass housing and then out the horn. *No one else can make sounds like this*, I thought.

If you've never played the instrument that God has designed specifically for you, a rich experience awaits you.

Know this!

- It produces a sound like no other
- Others may not appreciate it
- It will take you a while to master it
- It is needed for the richness of God's orchestra
- When you see the smile on the director's face as he points his baton at you, you'll realize your purpose

Exercising your special abilities can impact hundreds, thousands or even millions of people who sit in the audience of your life. You make a difference! Your sound is needed! No matter what you have done with your life to this point, there remains for you an opportunity to play your notes in a way that will affect the listeners.

It doesn't matter whether your parents rejected you, your peers ridiculed you or your spouse abandoned you. Even if you have lived what you would consider to be a meaningless or self-serving life up to this point, God has called you to rehearsal. He has written your name on His hand (Isaiah 49:16), the sound of your voice is on His lips (Isaiah 43:1) and your activities are on His mind (Psalm 115:12). Your identity is known and your influence is needed.

For years my son lived in Manhattan. On frequent visits I would find myself in Times Square. Looking around at the indistinguishable mass of humanity, I had to remind myself that God sees everyone. To Him every face is different, every expression a story, every life a song waiting to be played.

The things that you feel inside are not random, useless imaginings. They are part of a built-in dream that God has given you to pursue. Those flashes of insight that contain information about what you want to do, how you want to do it, and what kind of person you want to become in the process are a part of your Divine destiny. Like the genetic information inside a seed, your dreams and desires are actually a part of your spiritual "DNA" and they provide the very blueprint for your direction in life.

Will you dare to examine your God-given dream? It is characterized by those things that draw you, not drive you. A God-given dream is like a magnet exercising its attraction on your heart. Your dream provides the distinct and legitimate reasons for your passing through this life. Don't be lured away from it, but look on it. Examine it carefully. Then submit it to God.

The first step in reaching our dreams is to begin a relationship with the dream-giver. God created the world we live in and anticipated our presence in it. For us to achieve His purpose, we must accept His plan for the salvation of the world. The Bible says apart from Jesus we cannot do anything. Without Him you might follow a dream or idea for your life that God never intended. Some people dream of being rich or of exercising power over others, or of living a pleasure-filled lifestyle. But dreams are not from God if they don't fit within His plan for the earth as described in the Bible.

Here are some characteristics of a God-given dream:

- It fills a need
- It requires sacrifice
- It will outlive you
- It's irrepressible (it won't go away)
- It's huge (more than you can do alone)
- It draws attention to God's purposes

The Bible is filled with great men and women who realized God-given dreams. Noah, Abraham, Joseph, Moses, David, Daniel, Stephen, and even Christ himself had dreams that would powerfully impact human history. There are modern-day dreamers as well. You can become one of them. You are not one in a million. You are one among 8 billion. But you must play your part.

Over a century ago David Livingston read these words penned by Robert Moffat: "From where I stand, I can see the smoke of ten thousand African villages that have never heard of Christ."

Like an encounter with a burning bush, those words ignited a dream in Livingston's heart. As a result, he traveled 11,000 miles on foot through uncharted jungles. He was wracked by disease, attacked by wild animals, menaced by hostile tribes, and even robbed by his own carriers. Yet he marched on with his Bible. He preached the truth and fought slavery, until he won the heart of a nation and planted the seeds of emancipation in both Britain and America – all because he had a dream!

What is your dream? You may have dismissed it or taken a detour. It's time to revive it.

REFLECTION

1. What age were you (20s, 30s, 40s, 50s, etc.) when you finally concluded you had life figured out? How did you start to live differently?
2. Why isn't age a factor in discovering your Divine Design?
3. When you first realized God had something special for you to do in the world, how did you react to the news?
4. After we discover a dream that may be from God, why is it important that we surrender it back to Him?
5. Review Philippians 2:13. Describe how to figure out what part of God's work is from you and what part is from Him.

CHAPTER 6

YOUR UNIQUE SHAPE

Instead of trying to reshape yourself to be like someone else, you should celebrate the shape God has given you.
— Pastor Rick Warren

Anyone who has sat at a sidewalk café or on a park bench for hours, watching the stream of life passing by, knows the infinite variety of humankind. Sitting in a restaurant or an airport lounge or on a bus or train, or even gazing from the window of your office or study and observing the mini-dramas that unfold helps us understand that human behavior and human personality are infinitely diverse.

God loves variety. Did you know that in one cubic foot of snow there are 18 million snowflakes? And in those 18 million snowflakes not one is identical to another. No one except scientists seems to even notice or care, but God does. He could have made us all alike, but an original is worth more than a copy. You are valuable. You have been designed with a purpose.

It is God's plan that every day of your life should contribute to your Divine destiny. Isaiah 64:8 (NLT) states, "You are our Father. We are the clay, and you are the potter. We are all formed by Your hand." As we submit to God's purpose in creating us, His hands lovingly mold us into our specific shape. Rick Warren has brought worldwide attention to this idea with his popular S.H.A.P.E. acrostic. He writes, "Whenever God gives us an assignment, He always equips us with what we need to accomplish it. This custom combination of capabilities is called your S.H.A.P.E."

The concept of your SHAPE contains five specific characteristics:
• **Spiritual Gifts:** These are a set of special spiritual abilities given by God to help you serve others and share His love
• **Heart:** This consists of the special passions God has given you that motivate your service
• **Abilities:** These are inborn talents that are to be used to accomplish a specific God-defined purpose
• **Personality:** This special wiring affects how you see life and how you respond to circumstances
• **Experiences:** These are the positive and painful experiences of the past, which teach us lessons that can now be used for the benefit of others[1]

It would be unwise to try to understand our shape without consulting our Maker. After all, He is the One who fashioned us. We see this most clearly in the message God gave to Jeremiah.

> "Go down to the shop where clay pots and jars are made. I will speak to you while you are there." So I did as He told me and found the potter working at his wheel. But the jar he was making did not turn out as he had hoped, so the potter squashed the jar into a lump of clay and started again. Then the Lord gave me this message: "O Israel, can I not do to you as this potter's done to this clay? As the clay is in the potter's hand, so are you in My hand." Jeremiah 18:1-6 (NLT)

We see that we are to be clay in the Potter's hand. His responsibility is to shape us according to our intended function, and our responsibility is to remain soft and pliable so that He can mold us. He has given us abilities, interests, talents, gifts, personality and life experiences that are to be used according to our unique design. The Bible says our design is "wonderfully complex" and can never be duplicated. A careful understanding of our design will keep us from trying to conform, compare, compete or compromise our purpose. Instead we are to contribute to God's Kingdom in a way that pleases Him and serves others.

I have a friend who is a potter. His studio is in his home, and a trip to his workshop is a delight. Piece after piece, on shelf after shelf, stand the glazed treasures of his creativity. According to Mike, it's impossible to create two pieces with exactly the same design. The speed of the wheel, the arch of the hand, the hue of the glaze, the temperature of the kiln, and the length of its firing all have an impact on the end result. Mike has demonstrated his skills before church groups, comparing the process of making a piece of pottery to God making us. "How silly it would be," Mike would say, "for one pot to compare itself to another. Each one has its own form and purpose."

When I ask Mike about one of his creations, I am surprised at the level of detail he can share. His face is animated as he describes its uniqueness, its purpose, even its cracks and flaws. I have some of Mike's pottery in my kitchen. As I turn a piece over in my hands I think to myself, *I can never understand this piece as well as its creator.*

You and I need God (the Master Potter) to help us figure out the way we've been shaped. Without an understanding of our SHAPE, we end up doing things for which we were not designed in ways that don't work. The energy it takes to function outside our design is enormous. The frustration it brings to both us and others is tragic. And the result is always disappointing. That's what the animals that went to school discovered:

> Once upon a time, the animals decided they would do something meaningful to meet the problems of the new world. So they organized a school.
>
> They adopted an activity curriculum of running, climbing, swimming and flying. To make it easier to administer the curriculum, all the animals took all the subjects.
>
> The duck was excellent in swimming; in fact he was better than his instructor. But he made only passing grades in flying and was very poor in running. Since he was slow in running, he had to drop swimming and stay after school to practice running. This caused his webbed feet to be so badly worn he became only average in swimming. But average was quite acceptable, so nobody worried about that – except the duck.
>
> The rabbit started at the top of his class in running but developed a nervous twitch in his leg muscles because of so much make-up work in swimming.
>
> The squirrel was excellent in climbing, but he encountered constant frustration in flying class because his teacher made him start from the ground up instead of from the treetop down. He developed a charley horse from over-exertion, and so only got a C in climbing and a D in running.
>
> The eagle was a problem child and was severely disciplined for being a non-conformist. In climbing classes he beat all the others to the top of the tree but insisted on using his own way to get there.[2]

The lessons here are obvious. God created each animal with a unique design to accomplish a distinct purpose. Each is an expression of God's unique craftsmanship and should focus on its unique abilities.

When you use your unique SHAPE to fulfill your life purpose, not only is it fulfilling, but it draws attention to your Creator. It brings glory to God. That's what He had in mind all along.

REFLECTION

1. Have you ever felt that God might be prompting you to dream bigger dreams for Him? If so, how did you respond? What were the results?

2. Review the elements of your SHAPE. Which ones are easiest for you to identify? Which ones are the hardest to identify? Why are all important?

3. If, according to Jeremiah 18, we are clay in the Potter's hand, why do so many of us try to "remake" ourselves?

4. Review the animal story above. What "other species" are you most likely to imitate? Why do you think you have this tendency?

5. Explain how Jeremiah 2:3 might relate to using or not using your unique design.

CHAPTER 7

UNDERSTANDING SPIRITUAL GIFTS

Christ has generously divided out His gifts to us.
— Ephesians 4:7 (CEV)

S H A P E

When you mention spiritual gifts to some people, it's almost as though they expect the theme song from *The Twilight Zone* to begin playing. But spiritual gifts are neither eerie nor mystical. They aren't even complicated.

In a recent survey, George Barna asked American adults whether they knew of their spiritual gifts. Of those who had heard of spiritual gifts, fewer than one-third could correctly name even one gift. Less than a quarter could name a single one of their own spiritual gifts.[1] What a disadvantage for today's church.

The Bible is straightforward. A spiritual gift is simply a God-given ability to accomplish God's purpose on earth in a particular way. According to I Corinthians 2:14 these gifts are given only to those who have asked Jesus Christ into their life (after all, why would a person need an ability to accomplish God's purpose if he or she is not a God follower?).

These spiritual abilities are called *gifts* because no one earns or deserves them. They are not distributed on the basis of a person's educational background, family heritage, culture or economic status. If you grew up in a Christian family, you should know that simply because your mother had the gift of compassion and your father had the gift of service, that's no guarantee that you are going to be a Mother Teresa!

God alone determines which gift or gifts you will have, and there is no gift that is given to everyone.[2] Nor is there a single person walking this earth who has all of God's gifts. The reason is quite simple. If you had every gift, you would have no need of anyone else. And God's work in the world is a symphony, not a solo performance.

Paul compares gift distribution with arrangement of members in the physical body. How silly the body would look and how impractical it would be if it were made up of only an eye, or just a hand. God wants us to depend on each other so that His gifts flow through us as gifts to others. What we receive we pass on. "A spiritual gift is given to each of us as a means of helping the entire church," says Paul in I Corinthians 12:7 (NLT).

The Bible does not explain why certain gifts are given to certain people, but God's plan is for us to be sure that we have the resources that will enable us to get all of His Kingdom work done. When we don't use our gifts, or use them selfishly, we cheat the rest of humankind. That is why it's critical that we discover and develop our gifts to maximize the benefit to God and others.

My father grew up in a large family. Each Christmas Eve all the aunts, uncles, brothers, sisters, cousins, nieces and nephews gather for the same ritual. Inexpensive gifts are exchanged. In an attempt to make the process fair, numbers are distributed, and the higher your number, the less likely you are to get a gift that's meaningful. (You could possibly even receive a "regifted" item.) One particular Christmas I was at the bottom of the list. The gift left had a familiar shape; I had no doubt that it was some cheap men's aftershave. Shaking the box to confirm my suspicion, I took it home still wrapped. Since I had no need for any grooming products at the time, I laid it aside.

I didn't give it another thought until I came across the box in my closet several months later and my curiosity got the best of me. I tore the package open only to discover that I was the proud owner of a portable air compressor! Here's the irony. For weeks I had been checking stores for this particular item! There it was, doing no one any good because it remained wrapped.

How often we Christians make the same mistake. Not understanding or appreciating the shape of our gift, we leave it wrapped and unused. Whenever you receive a gift, you have to take the time to unwrap it. You can't use something when you're not sure what it is.

What are the gifts God offers? The Bible lists the following gifts specifically, but there's no reason to believe that this list is exhaustive:

- Administration – this is a special God-given ability to serve and strengthen the church that enables one to organize resources to reach ministry goals (I Corinthians 12:28)
- Apostleship – this God-given special ability allows the individual to strengthen the church by serving as a point leader for new ministry

ventures. (*Apostle* literally means "one sent with authority.") (I Corinthians 12:28)

- Discernment – the God-given special ability to help those in the church recognize truth and error within a message, person or situation (I Corinthians 12:10)
- Encouragement – the God-given special ability to serve the church by helping others live God-focused lives through the inspiration, encouragement and empowerment of another (Romans 12:8)
- Evangelism – the God-given special ability to serve the church by building a bridge of love to the unchurched in a way that helps people to respond (Ephesians 4:11-14)
- Faith – the God-given special ability to strengthen the church with a special ability to believe in God's purposes and trust Him to handle obstacles along the way to new objectives (I Corinthians 12:9)
- Giving – the God-given special ability to strengthen the church by supporting and funding Kingdom initiatives through material contributions beyond the tithe (Romans 12:8)
- Healing – the God-given special ability to serve and strengthen the body of Christ by serving the sick through prayers of faith that bring health and healing beyond traditional or natural means (I Corinthians 12:9, 28)
- Helping – the God-given special ability to serve the church by offering assistance in reaching goals in any way that accomplishes God's purpose (Romans 12:7, 28)
- Hospitality – the God-given special ability to strengthen the body of Christ by providing others with a warm and welcoming environment to facilitate friendship and fellowship (Romans 12:13)
- Tongues – the God-given special ability to strengthen the church by communicating God's message in a language unknown to the speaker (I Corinthians 12:10)
- Interpretation – the God-given special ability to serve the church by bringing understanding at a specific time to God's message spoken in another language and unknown to those in attendance (I Corinthians 12:10)
- Knowledge – the God-given special ability to strengthen the church by communicating God's truth to others in a way that promotes justice, honesty and understanding (I Corinthians 12:8)

- Leadership – the God-given special ability to serve the church by casting vision, stimulating spiritual growth, applying strategies for effectiveness and achieving goals where God's purposes are concerned (Romans 12:8)
- Mercy – the God-given special ability to serve the body of Christ by offering understanding and help to those who suffer physically, emotionally, spiritually or relationally; actions here are characterized by love, care, compassion and kindness (Romans 12:8)
- Miracles – the God-given special ability to strengthen the church through supernatural acts that validate God's power and involvement in the world (I Corinthians 12:10, 28)
- Pastoring – this God-given special ability allows an individual to strengthen the church by taking spiritual responsibility for a group of believers and helping to equip and train them to live God-centered lives. (This gift is sometimes referred to as "shepherding.") (Ephesians 4:11-12)
- Prophecy – the God-given special ability to strengthen the church by offering messages from God that comfort, encourage, guide, warn or reveal sin in a way that leads to repentance and growth (*Prophesy* literally means "to speak forth the truth." It includes both "forth-telling" [preaching] and "fore-telling" [revelation]) (I Corinthians 12:28)
- Teaching – the God-given special ability to strengthen the church by communicating sound Bible doctrine in relevant ways that empower people to apply the truth and grow spiritually (I Corinthians 12:28)
- Wisdom – the God-given special ability to strengthen the body of Christ through wise decisions and advising others with biblical truth (I Corinthians 12:8)[2]

These gifts from God are always to be used in a positive way. The Bible says they are given to strengthen and build up the church as a whole (I Corinthians 12:4-7). Every gift is to be expressed in love (I Corinthians 13) and used to the benefit of others (Matthew 25:35-40). No one gift is better than the others, though it may seem like certain gifts are more in demand based upon the need of the moment.

The purpose of your life is to take your God-given gifts and, through service, accomplish God's purpose on earth (Ephesians 4:11, 12). By doing so, you move from self-centeredness to a focus on others. W. H. Atken prayed, "Lord, take my lips and speak through them; take my mind and think through it; take my heart and set it on fire." Whatever gifts God has given us we must dedicate, along with ourselves, back to Him.

REFLECTION

1. Do you do most things because you "have to" or because you "choose to"?

2. Someone suggested that "… if you see yourself as a hammer, you view every project as a nail." What are the dangers of this approach to life?

3. Why do you think so many people leave God's gifts "unopened"? What effect do you think this has on the "gift" Giver?

4. Review the gifts listed above. Identify the top three gifts you believe you have. Ask a trusted friend if he or she agrees. Are you employing these gifts in God's service?

5. Read Paul's words in Philippians 3:14. It doesn't take any work to receive a gift, yet apparently it takes a good bit of work to succeed with it. Can you explain this?

CHAPTER 8

PUTTING SPIRITUAL GIFTS TO WORK

Each of you should use whatever gift you have received to serve others,
faithfully administering God's grace in its various forms.
— I Peter 4:10 (TNIV/NIV)

S H A P E

Spiritual gifts are not something to place on the mantel of our lives and admire. They are expressions of God's work through us and often are perceived as gifts only in retrospect. Since our strengths come easy to us, it isn't until someone points one out that we recognize we have done something unique.

For example, my wife didn't know she had the gift of encouragement until she started getting feedback from others about how much her words meant to them. My daughter didn't realize she had the gift of compassion until we started discussing why she was drawn to individuals with sometimes overwhelming needs.

Knowing our spiritual gifts can help steer us in the right direction, but it isn't until we attempt to use our gifts that we can really determine what God has given us. Did you ever volunteer for a responsibility or ministry and find out that it wasn't a good match for you? Perhaps you were given the assignment of making telephone contacts but you hate to talk on the phone. Or you were asked to organize the curriculum for a children's class and it was a total disaster. On the other hand, perhaps you found yourself being drawn to a disabled person or someone who was mentally impaired. While you were drained after a phone call or two or a little bit of filing, it seemed like you could spend all night showing love and care to others who weren't even part of your social network.

Unfortunately many churches attempt to place people in ministry without regard to their unique gifting. They use the old "Buffalo Bill" theory of lassoing the one that was too slow to get away. As a result people get frustrated and drop out of their responsibility.

Imagine if you were leading an orchestra and you let the members select whatever instruments they thought they might like to play. While drummers might be great at keeping a beat, they decide they'd like to sit in the front row and be flutists. Meanwhile, a trombone player feels like he might get more attention if he had sticks in his hand instead of a slide. A clarinetist wants to try the tuba and a saxophonist wants to play the French horn. Can you imagine the cacophony that would emerge? The members' skills do not fit their selected instruments.

Or imagine if the orchestra leader decided to move a piccolo player to the timpani. "Borrow an extra piccolo and you can use them for drumsticks," the leader might say. "No cymbals? No problem. We'll just crash two trumpets into each other." Can you imagine the chaos? None of us would participate in such an orchestra. Yet, too often, this is how we do church – volunteering ourselves without regard for our gifts or asking people to serve without finding out what each one does best. God has a better plan.

Listen to Paul sorting out the confusion about gifts that existed in the Corinthian Church:

> For no matter how significant you are, it is only because of what you are a part of. An enormous eye or gigantic hand wouldn't be a body, but a monster. What we have is one body with many parts, each its proper size and in its proper place. No part is important on its own. Can you imagine Eye telling Hand, "Get lost; I don't need you"? Or, Head telling Foot, "You're fired; your job has been phased out"? As a matter of fact, in practice it works the other way – the "lower" the part the more basic, and therefore necessary. You can live without an eye, for instance, but not without a stomach. The way God designed our bodies is a model for understanding our lives together as a church: every part dependent on every other part, the parts we mention and the parts we don't, the parts we see and the parts we don't. If one part hurts, every other part is involved in the hurt, and in the healing. If one part flourishes, every other part enters into the exuberance. (MES)

The obvious point here is that the gifts that God gives are for a purpose. All are necessary, and their use should not induce pride or jealousy.

But gifts are of no value unless they are tied to a specific role. In other words, we have to have a "place" of service. And God, as a Master Craftsman, desires to place you in the right role as He builds His church. If you are a hammer, and hammers are needed, then that is the part of the construction project where you belong. If you are a screwdriver, don't try to compete with the hammers. You'll do damage to yourself and the project. If you're a level, don't try to fit yourself into the edge of a screw. Not only will you become frustrated, but those around you will too.

The Bible says that every believer receives at least one gift (I Peter 4:10). Yet the biblical evidence indicates that some, if not most, have multiple gifts. For example, Paul identifies at least three gifts of his own in II Timothy 1:11. When finding a place for service, it may be helpful to recognize that many believers have a particular gift mix. And remember, the gifts combine beautifully for the purpose for which they've been given. One person might have a gift mix of leadership, administration, teaching and evangelism. That's an excellent gift mix to lead a church or ministry. Another person might have a gift mix of mercy, service and encouragement, which is an excellent mix to pray for the sick or counsel those having problems.

Give some thought to your gifts. Ask those around you, who may have more experience, what they see in you. Paul tells us in I Corinthians 12:1 that he doesn't want us to have a misunderstanding about our gifts. But we can't really understand them until we practice using them.

Find a church that believes in the importance of spiritual gifts and organizes itself around the gifts of its people. Then get started serving and evaluate your level of fulfillment and fruitfulness.

REFLECTION

1. In what areas have you taken on a responsibility only to discover you didn't have the innate resources to fulfill it? What steps did you take to rectify the situation?
2. Why do you think some gifts are more popular than others? Which ones do you tend to think of as more important than the rest?
3. Respond to this statement derived from I Corinthians 12: "You are only significant as a part of something greater."
4. Does your personal "gift mix" give hints about your Divine destiny? What are they?
5. Read I Timothy 4:14. Why do you think these words from Paul to this young leader were so important?

CHAPTER 9

UNDERSTANDING HEART

We may affirm absolutely that nothing great in the world has been accomplished without passion.
— Hegel, Philosophy of History, 1832

S H A P E

Heart, or passion, is the second piece to your life puzzle and very often marks the difference between a life of complacency and one marked by energy and excitement. Your heart's passion is what keeps you awake at night. When you experience it, you lose track of time. Athletes refer to it as being in the zone. Musicians call it flow. The Greeks coined a term to describe this feeling. They called it *eudaimonia*, which translates as "the feeling of giving your best where you have the best to give, and of reaping the rewards of this excellence." Whatever we label it, it holds the key to our happiness and a fruitful and fulfilling existence.

Everyone's heart beats for some purpose. What about yours? There's nothing quite as exhilarating as getting out of bed in the morning, going back into the world, and knowing why. Our hearts shine the light of passion upon some dreams or desires. These are hardwired into our souls and God intends for us to focus on them. Rick Warren puts it this way in *The Purpose Driven Life*:

> Physically, each of us has a unique heartbeat, just as we each have unique thumbprints, eye prints, and voice prints . . . It's amazing that, out of all the billions of people who have ever lived, no one has had a heartbeat exactly like yours.
>
> In the same way, God has given each of us a unique emotional "heartbeat" that races when we think about the subjects, activities, or circumstances that interest us.
> We instinctively care about some things and not about others. These reveal the nature of your heart . . . [and] are clues to where you should be serving.[1]

If you follow the path of your design, you are going to find that there are certain driving forces in your life. They affect the way that you direct your energies, use your time and focus your thoughts. In fact, your God-given passion serves as an internal guidance system for your life. Follow it and you will find satisfaction and fulfillment. We actually interpret reality in a way that suits the pattern of our heart. We tend to see life in terms of what has meaning for us in light of our gifts, passions and abilities.

Take time to notice where your interests lie in the midst of your busy life. What do you love enough to do for free? What gives you so much enjoyment that you yearn to do more of it? What were your childhood dreams? What do you get the biggest kick out of doing – even if you're not that great at doing it? What makes you feel best about yourself? When you daydream, where does your heart go? What brings the biggest grin to your face? What puts a spring in your step or a hum in your voice or a sparkle in your eyes? What gives you goose bumps? Your heart's passion really isn't that difficult to uncover when you consider these questions.

Here are some examples of what some identify as their heartbeat or passion:

Acquire/possess: I love to shop, collect, or obtain things. I enjoy getting the highest quality for the best price.

Design/develop: I love to make something out of nothing. I enjoy getting something started from scratch.

Excel: I love to be the best and make my team the best. I enjoy setting and attaining the highest standard.

Follow rules: I love to operate by policies and procedures. I enjoy meeting the expectations of others.

Improve: I love to make things better. I enjoy taking some thing others have designed or started and improving it.

Influence: I love to convert people to my way of thinking. I enjoy shaping the attitudes and behaviors of others.

Organize: I love to bring order out of chaos. I enjoy organizing something that is already started.

Perform:	I love to be on stage and receive the attention of others.
Persevere:	I love to see things to completion. I enjoy persisting in something until it's finished.
Pioneer:	I love to test and try out new concepts. I am not afraid to risk failure.
Prevail:	I love to pray for what is right and oppose what is wrong. I enjoy overcoming injustice.
Repair:	I love to fix what is broken or out of date.
Serve/help:	I love to assist others in their responsibility. I enjoy helping others succeed.
Take charge:	I love to lead the way, oversee, and supervise. I enjoy determining how things will be done.[2]

Of course there are many more. What might be yours?

Psalm 33:13-15 (NIV) states, "The Lord looks from heaven; He sees all humanity. From the place of His dwelling He looks on all the inhabitants of the earth; He fashions their hearts individually; He considers all their works."

Sometimes we'll say of someone, "When God made you He threw away the mold," but really that is true of all of us. You are a custom design. Isaiah 43:7 (MES) states that He "personally formed and made each one." You have no replacement and you can't return yourself to God's store for another model. You are it. And if you aren't you, the world misses out.

Over a century ago, Benjamin Disraeli said, "People achieve greatness only when they act from their heart and their passion. Those who learn to recognize the promptings of their heart and then find the courage to follow them are the ones who will be at the front of every race, at the head of every nation, as the author or artist behind every great masterpiece."[3]

Our heart guides our motivation. And these motivational patterns do not change over time. Nor do they change even after conversion. Consultants Mattson and Miller write:

> Our evidence demonstrates that motivational patterns do not change when a person becomes a Christian. The ingredients seen prior to conversion are seen after conversion. This is disturbing to people who expect it to be otherwise, but perhaps we will better

understand our position in Christ if we see that God's intention for us is not replacement of who we are, but redemption of who we are. God's creation of us, including our basic motivational pattern, is not bad . . . Conversion has us rejoicing in the fact that we are enabled to become who we originally were made to be, rather than becoming someone entirely different.[4]

The Bible uses the term *heart* to refer to that package of desires, hopes, interests, ambitions, dreams and affections that are uniquely you. Our service to God and others is to be done not only out of duty but out of passion. The Bible tells us that we are to serve the Lord our God with all our heart.[5] When considering service possibilities, it would be wise to give attention to our natural interests and intense desires.

When we serve God from the heart, we'll not only be enthusiastic but we'll also be effective. It turns out that whatever God wired us to love to do, we do well and enjoy improving. We might say that our passion drives us to the point of perfection. If you don't care about something, you are probably not going to be good at it. But if you do, you will keep working at it, constantly improving along the way.

Don't be afraid to use your heart motivations as part of God's internal guidance system for your life. It's all part of your design.

REFLECTION

1. What areas of your life are driven by the strongest passion?
2. What passion do you admire in others? Is it possible you notice in others what is important to you?
3. Think of a passion you once had but lost. Why do you think that happened?
4. What ways have you found to stimulate your heart toward God's purposes?
5. Read James 1:23-25. Describe the mirror you've been using to judge yourself. Does it have a crack in it? If so, how does an understanding of your passion help to repair it?

CHAPTER 10

PUTTING YOUR HEART TO WORK

As a face is reflected in water, so the heart reflects the person.
— Proverbs 27:19 (NLT)

S **H** A P E

A 13th-century Sufi poet wrote, "Let the beauty we love be what we do." The passion of our heart must have an object. It is the second piece of our identity puzzle, and it works alongside our spiritual gifts. It may include people such as the unchurched, the unborn or the poor, or it might include an issue such as family, civil rights or the right to life. Perhaps it has to do with a condition such as abuse or addiction or oppression. It might be focused on a specific place such as rural areas or third-world countries or major cities.

Paul had a passion for the Gentiles, and Peter had a passion for the Jews (Galatians 2:7). We talk about those who have a heart for children or for teens or for singles or for the elderly. When we combine our spiritual gifts with our heart's passion, it narrows the focus of our attention. For example, the gift of teaching may not serve for every age group at every time in every situation. A gift of teaching may be expressed to junior high boys because that is who a person has a heart for. It's okay to go for broke in the area of your heart.

Remember Jesus' two-sentence story in Matthew 13:45-46? He said, "The Kingdom of Heaven is like a merchant on the lookout for choice pearls. When he discovered a pearl of great value, he sold everything he owned and bought it!"(NLT) Here's a guy who spent his life as a pearl merchant. He had seen the very best. One day a diver pulls him aside and whispers, "I have the greatest pearl you've ever seen."

No doubt the merchant chuckled and thought, *That's what they all say.* The diver pulls him into the shadow of a nearby building and pulls the small cloth out of his pocket. As he opens the folds, the shimmering prize comes into view. It's unlike anything he's ever seen. The merchant closes the man's hand around the cloth and instructs him not to show his prize to anyone. The merchant promises to come back, ready to pay his asking price.

The pearl dealer liquidates everything – sells his house, his furnishings, his flocks and herds, even his favorite fishing boat, not to mention all those other pearls. He takes all the money and returns to take ownership of one pearl. Just one. But he valued it above all else. And with that purchase he gained his heart's desire.

When you are in touch with your heartfelt passion, that's exactly how you will think and live. You will be willing to risk all to pursue your heart's desire. It may take some time for you to get to the point where you understand what is most important, but don't let that stop you from getting started. Don't wait to begin using your passion until you understand all the details about it. Irwin McManus, in his book *Seizing Your Divine Moment*, states:

> Don't look for God to fill in all the blanks. Don't wait for Him to remove all the uncertainty. Realize He may actually increase the uncertainty and leverage all the odds against you, just so you will know in the end that it wasn't your gifts, but His power through your gifts, that fulfilled His purpose in your life.[1]

Your passion is going to push you to explore new horizons, to develop new relationships, and to seek solutions to difficult problems. So . . .

H – Highlight things that are important to you
E – Eliminate what you don't care about
A – Ask how you can help
R – Research your cause
T – Trust your passion

Tom Patterson writes, "Heart is where you were centered, where you desire to serve, the altar upon which you wish to place your talents. Giftedness is what you are. Heart is where you will most likely apply what you are. Heart refers to empathy, attraction, or 'draw' towards a group of people, a field of expertise, or a particular type of service. Evaluating your heart helps you determine where you might best use gifts, where you wish to serve, and whom you wish to serve."[2]

God wrote an adventure on your heart when He made you. You must decide whether you'll exchange a life of control that focuses on security or a life of faith filled with new challenges.

Consider the following:

1. If you were given permission to do what you really want to do, what would that be? (Start making a list of great and small deeds.) At this point, focus on the what, not the how.

2. What makes you come alive? If you could do what you've always wanted to do, what would it be?

3. What God-centered dreams can you identify that are buried within the recesses of your life?

4. Who could you ask for wisdom, support and encouragement as you identify your life's passions?

5. Identify two action steps you could take in the next week to let your heart beat for God.

One person with passion is greater than the force of 99 who only have interest. Henri Frederic Amiel said that "Without passion man is a mere latent force and a possibility, like a flint which awaits the shock of the iron before it can give forth its spark."[3]

Whatever needs you naturally desire to meet give clues to revealing your Divine destiny. Pursue them. And don't be surprised if your passion makes a deep impression on others. People are attracted to passion like moths to a flame. When you begin to act in passion, people will follow you.

Have you ever turned on your television but left the sound off? It's surprising how much you understand. People literally see what someone else is expressing. Passion is the element that makes our intent clear. Follow your heart. It will lead you straight to your Divine Design.

REFLECTION

1. Do you tend to have a passion toward people, things or ideas? Is one better than the others?

2. Is it possible to pursue an ideal too passionately? If so, how would you know when you crossed the line?

3. How would you respond to a person who says he or she has no passions?
4. How do you help a person who seems passionate about things that have little long-term value?
5. Read I Corinthians 2:9. If we can't totally grasp all God has in store for us, what is the point of this verse?

CHAPTER 11

UNDERSTANDING ABILITIES

God has given each of us the ability to do certain things well.
— Romans 12:6 (NLT)

S H A P E

You are the only one in all of creation who has your set of abilities. You're not only special, you're rare. You're not only rare, you're one of a kind, and in any endeavor there's great worth in one of a kind. A. Whitney Griswold stated: "Could *Hamlet* have been written by a committee or the Mona Lisa painted by a club? Could the New Testament have been composed as a conference report? Creative ideas do not spring from groups. They spring from individuals. The divine spark leaps from the finger of God to the finger of Adam."[1]

No doubt you've been more aware of your natural, God-given abilities than any of your other design components. This piece of the puzzle is the easiest to figure out. Because these abilities are inborn, you've lived with them longer than your spiritual gifts (which are given at the time of salvation). It is also true that the world around you more easily spots these abilities than anything else in your design.

If you take a long, honest look at what you are good at and what you're not, chances are you will begin to see patterns of consistent behavior that reveal inborn skills and talents. Just review the important accomplishments, hobbies, jobs, interests and themes in your life to see these inborn Divine Design elements.

You may have natural athletic abilities. Or perhaps you are good at mechanics or music or mathematics.

Perhaps you are one of the fortunate individuals who discovered early on what you do best and have spent your life doing it! What you may not have realized is that these abilities come from God. Since they have been given by Him, they are just as important as your spiritual gifts.

You have unique and distinctive characteristics that have been woven through your life experience. You are not a bland generality. And when you learn to fully use the talents you have, people will call you talented.

If you were to draw a time line from the moment you were born until today, at what points did you feel most fulfilled and most recognized? What themes and patterns are revealed by the peak points in your life? What personal strengths do these reveal?

If you have an ability to teach you'll find someone to teach, even if it's only a collection of stuffed animals lined up against the headboard of a bed. If you have a talent as an entrepreneur, chances are it began showing up when you opened your first lemonade stand as a kid. An engineer can't help making little drawings and sketches that connect him to the world. A nurse will find someone to whom care can be rendered.

In Exodus 31:3 we see an example of God giving people "skill, ability and knowledge in all kinds of crafts" in order to fulfill His purpose. In this case, it was the artistic ability that was necessary to build the tabernacle.
I Corinthians 12:5 (NIV) says, "There are different kinds of service, but the same Lord."

It may surprise you to know that God wants you to use your abilities . . . for Him! After all, you are the only person on earth who can put your particular combination of abilities into play. No one else can take your place because they don't have the unique SHAPE that God has given you.

But, you ask, what if God has given me a passion for something but I seem to have little or no ability in it? Perhaps you have a yearning to do something, but no matter how often you do it, you don't seem to improve. These little diversions are called hobbies. Enjoy them! Have fun doing them, but don't let them siphon off energy from your truly productive areas.

And remember that what God has done for you, He has done for others. They, too, have unique abilities though they are certainly different from yours. It is unfair to expect "out" of people what God has not put "in." I remember receiving some good advice during a particularly frustrating time of trying to coach someone to do something that was not in their package of abilities. A friend counseled, "I've learned not to try to make a pig sing. You won't succeed, and you'll irritate the pig."

Sometimes people try to use their God-given abilities to make a name for themselves rather than try to fulfill God's purposes. The results can be very disappointing. Sports writer Gary Smith once interviewed boxing legend Mohammad Ali. The interview was concluded at the fighter's farmhouse, and during their time together, Ali took Smith on a tour of his estate. When he was led into the barn, the writer saw all of Ali's trophies, ribbons and awards on a shelf, collecting dust – some of them even spattered with pigeon droppings.

As they surveyed all the boxing memorabilia getting ruined, Mohammad Ali said something very quietly to Smith. He spoke so softly, in fact, that the writer had to ask him to repeat what he had said.

With his lips barely moving, the words seemed to come from the back of the champ's throat: "I had the world and it wasn't nothin'."[2]

Your abilities, no matter how great, are "nothing" if not put to their proper use. Use them as God intended. The way that you are wired is a great predictor for God's will for your life. Far too many people look at what's absent in their life instead of what they've been given. They say, "If only I had this, if only I had that, then I could really accomplish what God has for me." Too many people overestimate the importance of things they don't have and underestimate the importance of the things they do.

God has already given you what you need to begin to create a vastly improved future. The Bible says God provides us with "all we need for doing His will."[3] It's time to thank Him for it. Gratitude nourishes your Divine Design and opens you to accept the gifts and abilities you've been given. Thank God for them, figure them out, use them in service and keep developing them!

REFLECTION

1. Go back in time and think of the earliest affirmations you received for your abilities. Are these abilities still with you today? Why or why not?

2. Can you identify an ability that you may have buried because of the reaction of the people around you? What effect is that having?

3. What abilities are you using in your hobbies or career that might benefit the Kingdom of God? Who might help you accomplish that?

4. How will an understanding of God-given abilities affect what you will expect of others?

5. Read Jeremiah 9:23-24. Why does God scoff at the human measurements of success?

CHAPTER 12

PUTTING YOUR ABILITIES TO WORK

A vision without a task is but a dream,
a task without a vision is drudgery;
a vision and a task is the hope of the world.
— Inscription on an old English church

S H **A** P E

God does not have a giant photocopy machine or a divine replicator. He never makes copies of anything. No two parts of His creation are exactly the same, and you have no replacement. He only makes originals. So the talent combinations that exist in you have never been seen in the world, nor will they ever be seen after you're gone. That means you have a unique contribution to make.

What might it be?

Are you the woman with a flair for fashion and accessorizing?

Are you the working mother with a "genius" for balancing career and parenting?

Are you the enthusiastic biology student considered a "born scientist"?

Are you the proofreader who can spot a missing period from across the room?

Are you the bookkeeper with a knack for number crunching?

Are you the girl known as a "natural" for taking care of young children?

Are you the handyman with a gift for fixing anything?

Are you the waitress who everybody wants because of her ability to satisfy customers?

Are you the computer whiz who can make machines do the impossible?

Who are you really? We know something about you by looking at your abilities and talents. The problem is, we're much better at identifying our weaknesses than our strengths. But trying to over-improve our weaknesses can result only in strong weaknesses.

In various teaching settings I've asked the audience to take a few minutes and list all the things they're good at. The average number of responses is five. Then I ask the same group to take the same amount of time and list the things that they think they should improve on. I've seen lists as high as

50! We are much better at focusing on what's wrong with us than what's right.

Studies have shown that the average human being has between 500 and 800 abilities. In the Bible people were talented in everything from boat building to tent making. Since many of the abilities described in the Bible are for a different time and culture, allow me to list for you some of the kinds of abilities you may have:

- ☐ Achieving
- ☐ Administrating
- ☐ Arranging
- ☐ Calculating
- ☐ Classifying
- ☐ Competing
- ☐ Consulting
- ☐ Counseling
- ☐ Designing
- ☐ Developing
- ☐ Distributing
- ☐ Eliminating
- ☐ Engineering
- ☐ Filing
- ☐ Implementing
- ☐ Inspecting
- ☐ Leading
- ☐ Listening
- ☐ Motivating
- ☐ Operating
- ☐ Pioneering
- ☐ Promoting
- ☐ Researching
- ☐ Strategizing
- ☐ Traveling
- ☐ Writing

- ☐ Acting
- ☐ Analyzing
- ☐ Budgeting
- ☐ Charting
- ☐ Coaching
- ☐ Computing
- ☐ Cooking
- ☐ Deciding
- ☐ Detecting
- ☐ Directing
- ☐ Drawing
- ☐ Encouraging
- ☐ Establishing
- ☐ Fixing
- ☐ Improving
- ☐ Inspiring
- ☐ Learning
- ☐ Managing
- ☐ Navigating
- ☐ Performing
- ☐ Planning
- ☐ Recruiting
- ☐ Resourcing
- ☐ Teaching
- ☐ Visualizing
- ☐ Other

- ☐ Adapting
- ☐ Anticipating
- ☐ Building
- ☐ Checking
- ☐ Communicating
- ☐ Connecting
- ☐ Coordinating
- ☐ Decorating
- ☐ Determining
- ☐ Discovering
- ☐ Editing
- ☐ Enforcing
- ☐ Examining
- ☐ Forecasting
- ☐ Influencing
- ☐ Landscaping
- ☐ Lecturing
- ☐ Mentoring
- ☐ Negotiating
- ☐ Persuading
- ☐ Predicting
- ☐ Repairing
- ☐ Serving
- ☐ Translating
- ☐ Welcoming

Which of the above abilities do you think you might have? If you placed check marks next to the ones you see in yourself, you may have found that you are multitalented. (And there are many abilities not included on this list.) Since all of these abilities come from God, they can also be used by God. Your abilities will match the calling on your life. Sometimes you hear Christians say they feel "called" by God into ministry to become a missionary or pastor. But, according to the Bible, every believer is called by God into ministry. First, we're called to salvation and second, we're called to serve. One of the ways you know what you're called to, and how you're called to serve, is to examine your abilities.

God has made a tremendous investment in you. Will His investment bring a return? When He asks you one day, "What did you do with what you were given?" will you be able to say that you used your abilities to honor Him and serve others?

God intends for us to dedicate our abilities back to Him. Romans 12:1 (TEV) says: "Offer yourselves as a living sacrifice to God, dedicated to His service and pleasing to Him." If God has given us these abilities, then we must use them for His purpose, not for the wrong purpose. For example, you can be a talented teacher and teach criminals how to break into houses and commit robberies. There are brilliant criminals who use God-given abilities for selfish purposes.

The second thing we must do with our abilities is to cultivate them. In other words, we have to develop them, practice with them, improve them. Abilities are meant to be used in service to others. The Bible says in Ecclesiastes 10:10 (NIV): "If the axe is dull and its edge is unsharpened, more strength is needed. But skill will bring success."

How do you get skill? Through practice. Through sharpening your axe. Through working smarter rather than harder. What happens if I don't practice? Max Lucado writes in his book *Shaped by God*,

> To find me, look over in the corner of the shop, over here, behind the cobwebs, beneath the dust, in the darkness. There are scores of us, broken handles, dulled blades, cracked iron. Some of us were useful once and then . . . many of us never were. But, listen, don't feel sorry for me. Life ain't so bad here in the pile . . . no work, no anvils, no pain, no sharpening. And yet, the days are very long.[1]

The only way to develop your abilities is to use them. Get started today. No matter where you are in chronological age, God is not finished with you yet. Don't die until you're dead. Romans 11:29 (NIV) says: ". . . God's gift and His call are irrevocable." What God has put in you stays for your whole life and He wants you to use it to fulfill His plan. The more you do with what He has given you, the more you can do.

REFLECTION

1. If you were asked to give up all but three things that make you "you," what would those three things be?
2. Do you find yourself attracted to people who have the same abilities as you or those who have different abilities? Why do you think that may be?
3. Give an example of when you saw great ability run aground (no names please). How do you think this could have been prevented?
4. Can you think of a dramatic example of when you felt God's investment in your ability was squandered? How did you recover?
5. Read Hebrews 12:8. Why is discipline a prerequisite for discovering your Divine Design?

CHAPTER 13

UNDERSTANDING PERSONALITY

Like stained glass, our different personalities reflect God's light in many colors and patterns.
— Rick Warren

S H A $\boxed{P}$ E

The Bible makes it clear that our devotion to God must be total. In Mark 12:29 (NLT), Jesus tells us the most important commandment is for us to "Love the Lord your God with all your heart, all your soul, all your mind, and all your strength." In other words, God's plan for you is to do a lot more than check off items from a "to do" list. You are to love God and pursue His purposes with all of your being. Yet each human "being" is different. Each of us focuses on loving God more one way than another. This fits His plan perfectly because God wants you to love and serve Him with *your* personality. You will not do it in exactly the same way as anyone else. Maybe you'll do it more with your heart or more with your soul or more with your mind or more with your strength. How do you love God? More with your conversation, more with your feelings, more with your thinking, or more with your action?

Perhaps it would be easier to identify your personality by thinking in terms of your comfort zones. Here are some questions to ask yourself that might help.

Do you love the spotlight or shun it?
Do you enjoy being with people, or do you prefer being alone?
Do you like living with risks, or do you need to feel secure?
Do you enjoy taking a leadership role, or do you want to follow?
Do you like focusing on projects, or people?
Do you want to create a movement, or are you looking for your niche in someone else's design?
Do you like being singled out, or prefer to stand in the shadows?
Is your life motto "the end justifies the means," or do you need every step of the process to be justified?
Do you prefer being on the frontline or in the back-room?

Is the celebration of success as important to you as the success itself?

Are relationships more important to you than things or ideas?

When an idea is introduced, do you find yourself trying to understand the assumptions that went into it?

When you walk into a room do you find yourself saying "Here I am" or "There you are"?

The answers to those questions give you clues to your personality. None of the answers are right or wrong; they are just different.

One approach to understanding our personalities has been popularized by pastor and author Tim LaHaye. It is the ancient idea that there are four basic personality types.

Sanguine (soul people) – emotional and demonstrative
Choleric (heart people) – strong-willed, decisive, born leader
Phlegmatic (strength people) – easygoing, calm, well-balanced
Melancholy (mind people) – deep, thoughtful, analytical

These personality types are sometimes referred to as temperaments, and you can find examples of all of these types in the Bible. For example, Paul was a Choleric. Peter was a Sanguine. Moses was a Phlegmatic and Jeremiah was a Melancholy. None of these personality types are better or worse than the others. From God's perspective it takes all kinds of people to reach all kinds of people. Imagine a world where every flavor was plain vanilla. Yuck!

A very similar approach in personality discovery is used in the D.I.S.C. model. Here is a summary of the four main types:

D is the dominating, directing, driving, demanding, determined, decisive, doing personality that corresponds to the Choleric.

I is the inspiring, influencing, inducing, impressing, interactive, interested in people personality that corresponds to the Sanguine.

S is the steady, stable, shy, security-oriented, servant, submissive, specialist that corresponds to the Phlegmatic.

C is the cautious, competent, calculating, compliant, careful, contemplative personality that corresponds to the Melancholy.[1]

Mels Carbonell tells a cute story of the interplay of these various personalities in an elementary school classroom. The teacher asked the question "Who discovered America?" and the different personalities interact.

Rocky, the high "D" Choleric, yells out, "Columbus. Next question!" The teacher responds, "Why did you yell out like that, Rocky? Why don't you raise your hand like everyone else?"

Rocky likes to take charge. He wants to be in control. He wants to get everything done in a hurry so he can go play.

The teacher asks again, "Who discovered America?" Sparky, the high "I" Sanguine, jumps up, waving his hand, and says, "I know, I know. Call on me, teacher! Please!" She responds, "Okay, Sparky. Who discovered America?"

He acts like he knows but says, "Oh, I forgot. It's right on the tip of my tongue. Can you give me the first letter?" He wants to turn it into a game like Wheel of Fortune. He asks, "Can I buy a vowel?"

The teacher sighs, "Oh Sparky, put your hand down and stop acting like a clown. Why do you always raise your hand without having anything to say?"

Sparky responds with a surprised, silly face and sits down while the class laughs at his antics.

The teacher then asks Susie, the high "S," which corresponds to the Phlegmatic, "Who do you think discovered America?"

Softly Susie says, "I think it's Columbus, but I'm not sure. If anyone else knows and wants to say, it's okay with me. And if you don't like Columbus, I'm sorry. I hope my answer doesn't make anyone mad."

Finally the teacher asks Claire, the high "C," which corresponds to the Melancholy, "Do you know who discovered America?"

Claire gives the teacher one of those disgusting glares and blurts out, "Now what do you mean by that question?"

Rocky explodes, "Come on Claire! Why do you make a mountain out of a molehill? Let's finish this stuff so we can go out and play!"

Rocky loves recess. He considers himself king of the playground. He tells everybody, "We're going to play kickball today. I'm captain." And, pointing to a friend, says, "And you're captain of the other team."

Another strong-willed student interrupts, "I don't want to play kickball. Who made you captain anyway?" That's two of the same personalities challenging each other.

Sparky gets all excited. He says, "I love it when Rocky is about to get into a fight." Sparky yells, "Ding, round two" like the ring announcer at a boxing match.

Poor Susie covers her face and begins to cry. Sobbing, she says, "I'm sorry, I'm sorry. I didn't know it was going to upset anyone. Please forgive me and don't fight."

Finally Claire screams, "Now wait a minute! What about the Native American Indians? They were here before Columbus. What about the Vikings? They were here before Columbus. You need to be clearer with your question!"[2]

As you can see from the story, every child responds according to his or her personality. Each one has a somewhat predictable pattern of behavior. Chances are, you recognize the grown-up version of these personalities in the circle of your relationships. Which one are you most like?

None of us is precisely one personality. We are a blend. Florence Littauer says, "My temperament is the real me; my personality is the dress I put on over me." I can look in the mirror in the morning and see a plain face, straight hair, and a bulgy body. That's the real me. Gratefully within an hour I can apply makeup to create a colorful face; I can plug in the curling iron to fluff up my hair; I can put on a flattering dress to camouflage too many curves. I've taken the real me and dressed it up, but I haven't permanently changed what's underneath."[3]

We're a mix. We're a mesh. Your DNA molecules can unite in a nearly infinite number of ways. The number is 10 to the 2.4 billionth power. No wonder you'll never find anyone else just like you!

Take a look at some of the following personality traits and identify the ones that are most like you.

☐ Adaptable	☐ Adventurous	☐ Analytical
☐ Animated	☐ Balanced	☐ Bold
☐ Cheerful	☐ Competent	☐ Competitive
☐ Considerate	☐ Consistent	☐ Contented
☐ Controlled	☐ Convincing	☐ Daring
☐ Decisive	☐ Deep	☐ Demonstrative
☐ Detailed	☐ Diplomatic	☐ Faithful
☐ Forceful	☐ Friendly	☐ Funny
☐ Idealistic	☐ Independent	☐ Inoffensive

- ☐ Inspiring
- ☐ Lively
- ☐ Mixer
- ☐ Obliging
- ☐ Patient
- ☐ Persistent
- ☐ Playful
- ☐ Positive
- ☐ Refreshing
- ☐ Respectful
- ☐ Self-reliant
- ☐ Shy
- ☐ Spontaneous
- ☐ Sure
- ☐ Thoughtful

- ☐ Leader
- ☐ Loyal
- ☐ Mover
- ☐ Optimistic
- ☐ Peaceful
- ☐ Persuasive
- ☐ Pleasant
- ☐ Productive
- ☐ Reserved
- ☐ Satisfied
- ☐ Self-sacrificing
- ☐ Sociable
- ☐ Strong-willed
- ☐ Talker
- ☐ Tolerant

- ☐ Listener
- ☐ Mediator
- ☐ Musical
- ☐ Outspoken
- ☐ Perfectionist
- ☐ Planner
- ☐ Popular
- ☐ Promoter
- ☐ Resourceful
- ☐ Scheduled
- ☐ Sensitive
- ☐ Spirited
- ☐ Submissive
- ☐ Tenacious

The Bible says in I Corinthians 12:6 (PH) that "God works through different people in different ways, but it is the same God who achieves His purpose through them all." Everyone's personality is significant. There are no unimportant people. Make the most of yourself, for that is all that God made of you.

Too many people spend time and energy trying to imitate others rather than investing in their own development. They want to be able to write songs like Michael W. Smith, preach like Billy Graham or write like Max Lucado before they are willing to do anything. God knew what He was doing when He put you together. He intends for you to use what you possess. Your life makes a difference and although we are all different, no personality is insignificant.

God doesn't want you to be a clone of everyone else. He wants to strengthen your personality, not dampen it. He wants you to be more you than you've ever been before. Your personality is deeply personal.

Reflection

1. What type of personality have you most admired over the years? How close a match is this to your own personality?
2. Of the four basic personality types listed in this chapter, which type is most like how you see yourself? Do your responses to the list of traits match your selection?
3. Does your personality match the tasks you perform most often? How does that make you feel?
4. How do you respond to people of an opposite personality type? Is this opposite "type" most likely to help or harm you?
5. Read Luke 15. In these three stories there is a lost object. What are the parallels between the owner's joy at discovering what was lost and God's joy over your discovery of Him?

CHAPTER 14

PUTTING YOUR PERSONALITY TO WORK

The curious paradox is that when I accept myself just as I am, then I can change.

— Carl Rogers

S H A **P** E

Live your life as an exclamation, not an explanation. Why dream of the person you're supposed to be and, by doing so, waste the person that you are? The only life you have is your own. Why not live it? If you are going to walk in somebody else's tracks, you're never going to leave your own footprints, so be who you are. Most people live their entire lives as complete strangers to themselves. Don't let that happen to you.

A father and son were walking along the mountains. The boy stumbled and fell, hurting himself, and screamed: "Aaahhhhh!!!"

To his surprise, he hears a voice on the mountain repeating: "Aaahhhhh!!!" Curious, he yells: "Who are you?"

He receives the answer: "Who are you?"

Angered at the response, he screams: "Coward!"

He receives the answer: "Coward!"

He looks to his father and asks: "What's going on?"

The father smiles and says, "Pay attention son."

The man screams at the mountain: "I admire you!"

The voice answers: "I admire you!"

Again the man screams: "You are the best!"
The voice responds: "You are the best!"

The boy is surprised but does not understand.

Then the father explains: "People call this echo, but really this
is LIFE. It gives you back everything you say or do. Our life is
simply the echo of our actions. Life will give you back everything
you have given to it."[1]

Your life is a reflection of your belief about yourself.

If you believe you have value and something unique to contribute, you
will be busy giving it to the world. Your only resources are what you have,
not what you don't. Opportunity knocks where you are, never where you
were.

Your personality development may be a resource that you've mostly ne-
glected. In your attempt to imitate others you may have missed the beauty
of what you possess and the opportunity to use it to imitate Christ. Teddy
Roosevelt once stated: "Do what you can, with what you have, where you
are." Don't spoil what you've been given by neglecting it until it's too late.
No improvement is as certain as that which proceeds from the right and
timely use of what you already have. The inborn characteristics of your
personality present one of your greatest opportunities to discover your
Divine destiny. Because your temperament was prepackaged at birth, you
have a great start at discovering how God intends for you to relate to your
environment.

Your personality gives you two clues to life direction. The first is how
you relate to people and the second is how you relate to possibilities. According to the dictionary, your personality is the complex combination of
characteristics that distinguishes you from another. These unique God-
given behavioral characteristics affect the way you think, feel and act and
influence your entire life, whether you are conscious of it or not. Arthur F.
Miller, Jr., states:

Your life has meaning built into it. Effectively, you have an exciting, challenging, and achievable destiny if you will but discover
and embrace who you were designed to be.[2]

Think for a moment how you will use your personality as you relate to people. For example, when you bump into someone you don't know, do you see it as an opportunity to enrich your understanding or would you prefer to withdraw? One is not necessarily better than the other, but both should be recognized as different types of personalities. You may be outgoing or reserved. You might be very expressive or self-controlled. You might be cooperative or competitive.

How do you respond to possibilities? Do you like to focus on projects instead of people? Do you like low-risk or high-risk situations? Do you prefer to follow someone else or to lead them? Are you a team player, or do you like to function alone? Do you like routine or variety? Which setting is the best for you to express how you relate to others – one on one, in a small group, or in a large group? As you rate yourself on the continuum between these various extremes, you'll come closer to understanding the true you. Others can also help in the evaluation process, especially as we start using our personalities in service to others. You may ask for feedback, or it may come as the natural outgrowth of your service.

Have you ever thought about talking with your boss about how you might be able to better align your Divine Design and your work responsibilities? Hopefully your boss will realize that the more you play to your strengths, the more effective you will be. When I worked in the corporate world I volunteered for an assignment that was outside my job description. When my boss saw my effectiveness he asked me if I wanted to do the job permanently. I accepted, on the condition that I could give part of my current responsibility to someone else since it was not playing to my strengths. I suggested a coworker's name who loved to do what I loathed. It was a win for all of us.

Be careful not to fall in love so deeply with your personality that it becomes the standard against which you measure everyone. It is a tool to be used, not a trait to be idolized. C. S. Lewis writes fictionally of an artist who was separated from God because he eventually fell in love with his paint instead of the Light that was the source of his passion for painting in the first place. Lewis, through the character of Spirit, cautions:

> Every poet, musician and artist, but for Grace, is drawn away
> from the love of the thing he tells, to love of the telling til, down

in Deep Hell, they cannot be interested in God at all but only in what they say about Him. For it doesn't stop at being interested in paint, you know. They sink lower – become interested in their own personalities and then in nothing but their own reputations.[3]

Remember, your personality is to serve a purpose. We see this illustrated in the Bible each time God instituted a name change to highlight His plan for someone. In Genesis 17 God changed Abram's name to Abraham and Sarai to Sarah. Then in Genesis 32 we see Jacob's name changed to Israel. This is an interesting one because Jacob's birth name meant "schemer" or "hustler." Israel was his "discovered" name. A name given to him based on his new identity. In John 1:42 Jesus changed Simon to Cephas, which is translated as Peter the Rock. In Matthew 16 Peter's whole identity and specific purpose were revealed to him through his interaction with Jesus.

Each of these individuals better understood themselves and their destinies when they encountered God more personally and intimately. Suddenly they knew how to put their personalities to work. An understanding of your personality will come as you encounter Christ in new and deeper ways. He will call out your personality strengths and help you cope with your weaknesses. After all, it's all part of His design.

REFLECTION

1. What do you understand about how your personality was designed?
2. What difference does it make to know that your personality is purposeful rather than random?
3. What is your default? Do you find yourself relating more to people or to possibilities?
4. How could your personality be seen as a benefit in these random life situations?
   a) a crisis at work   b) a fight at home   c) a neighbor in difficulty
5. Read Psalm 149:14. How does this expression of praise remind us of our need to accept and cherish the personality God has given us?

CHAPTER 15

UNDERSTANDING EXPERIENCES

What might your past have prepared you to do that you couldn't — or wouldn't — do otherwise?
— Craig Groeschel

S H A P E

There's one last piece of the puzzle remaining in your examination of your SHAPE. It's the one you are most likely to have left out. It is your life experiences. When you unpack your bag on the journey of life, your experiences, particularly the difficult ones, are often tossed out like empty candy wrappers. After all, what good could there be in getting fired from your job, or experiencing an unwanted pregnancy, or being abused by a parent? Believe it or not, your past might be a key to unlocking your future.

In my garage I have a cabinet. In the cabinet is a shelf, on the shelf is a bowl and in the bowl are about 100 keys. They've been accumulating over the course of my lifetime. Some were duplicates. Some were keys to things I never used. Others looked too unusual to discard. After all, they might be important! I keep these keys just in case. Just in case I find an important door I cannot open.

What if I told you that you have a bowl of keys sitting on a shelf in your heart? Not keys to start a car or open a suitcase, but keys that could open the doors of understanding to your God-given design.

These keys are your past experiences – both good and bad. Some that you hope you'll never forget and others you hope you'll never remember.

As a pastor for over 30 years I've had a ringside seat to most of life's disasters – bankruptcies, wayward children, suicides, terminal illnesses, betrayals, abuses, and incarceration. In every case I can think of, those affected would have given anything to avoid the trauma. Yet, amazingly, many of them have turned their pain into something productive. You see, for the Christian, experiences have meaning. God somehow taps the kaleidoscope through which we view the world – and suddenly the image created by the cut pieces of glass looks entirely different.

David was still a teenager, fresh off of shepherding, when he faced his first giant in Goliath. But the Bible says he had had some important experiences that gave him the confidence and the courage to take on this big guy. David remembered when a bear attacked a sheep and God helped him kill it. Another time he was threatened by a lion and God gave him the strength for that, too.

Now I don't think that when David looked at his shepherd's crook and then looked at that hungry lion he thought to himself, *Hey, I'll be able to put this on my resume!* But later his past turned out to be a key to his future. David must have thought, *Hey, bear, lion, why not giant? God was with me then, He'll be with me now!*[1]

We don't just benefit from the struggles of life. We also benefit from its successes. Perhaps you overcame a health crisis and now you offer hope and help to others. Or perhaps you turned around a struggling company and now you teach others how to do so. Maybe you enjoy buying old houses and fixing them up or have an aptitude for picking stocks on the rise. Your successes have built confidence for you to do these things in greater ways that affect more people.

God wants you to embrace the experiences of your life – all of them. The good, the bad and the ugly. The right ones, the wrong ones, the happy and sad ones. If you run from your past, it will chase you your whole life. God wants to use it for good. But you've got to turn around, face it and give it to God. Do not waste experiences. Use them for something good.

Too many people let the past imprison them. As a little boy I was a witness to some animal cruelty I will never forget. On my first visit to a neighbor's house I was introduced to the family dog. It was kept outside and had its own house for shelter. I could tell by the well-beaten path along the line of his chain that he had been there for a long time. I asked my friend if they ever let him loose to run. "Oh no," he said. "He's too mean."

In typical little boy style he asked me if I wanted to see something gross. What young boy doesn't want to see something gross? In those days I lived for gross! But this gross was way out of my comfort zone. My friend took me to the very edge of the dog path and when the dog came close he said, "Look at his neck."

I couldn't believe my eyes. His chain was attached to a choker and the choker had cut into the dog's skin so deeply that scar tissue had begun to grow over it. I will never forget the sight. No wonder the dog was mean! Every movement must have meant pain.

I have seen the past fasten people's lives down with a chain. I have seen the past rub the neck of a life raw. I have watched the infected skin grow over the choking experience until there was no hope of release and it seemed like every step brought pain.

I'm sure that dog longed to be free but could no longer imagine the possibility. And even if he could have loosened the chain from its mooring, can you imagine the pitiful sight of him dragging the chain behind him, since the choker was still embedded in his skin? Many people who think they have broken free are actually still dragging the chain of their past with them – the woman who leaves her abusive husband to take up residence with a man who has an addiction, the man who sues his business partner to gain a windfall then loses it through gambling. These people are free from the stake that held them down but are still dragging their rusty chain with them. These people have the same pieces of the puzzle to their Divine Design that we have, but it is as though they are assembling the parts in a darkened room. Each piece is clumsily squeezed into place and then the edges are ground down so that they feel well positioned. But pull up the shades, let a little light into the room, and we can see the truth. Everything is out of place. It's just not right.

What makes the difference between a past that weighs us down and one that sets us free? Our attitude toward the past makes the difference. No one has the same past experiences you do, but all of us have hurt in our past. For these difficult experiences to be used as part of your Divine destiny, they must be surrendered to God. Where forgiveness is required, it must be given. Where reconciliation or restoration is needed, it must be offered.

Jesus said in John 10:10 that the thief (Satan) comes to steal and kill and destroy. Unforgiveness is the window through which he enters, and you are the only one who can close it! The word *forgive* literally means "to let go." It has nothing to do with the other person involved. It is a decision you make. Much like expelling carbon dioxide from your body, because you know holding on to it will only hurt you, you release it. Go ahead and exhale! And then let God use your past experience to help others. According to Romans 8:28 we know that God can use everything in our lives for the good. It doesn't mean that the experience is good, but He loves to bring good things out of bad situations. After all, He is the Master at turning crucifixions into resurrections. God can bring a message out of the messy experiences of your life. Why not let Him? It's all part of His plan for your Divine Design.

REFLECTION

1. If God intends our life experiences to affect our life purpose, explain what effect the accumulation of more and more experiences might have. Can you give an example?
2. Why was it necessary for God to reference David's experience when telling the story of David slaying Goliath?
3. What is God most likely to get more attention from – your tragedies or your triumphs? Why?
4. If God wants to use our past to help us serve in the present, why do you think so many Christians try to hide their past?
5. Read Colossians 3:1-4. How does this truth keep us from envying the experiences of others or regretting our own experiences?

CHAPTER 16

PUTTING YOUR EXPERIENCES TO WORK

Experience is not what happens to you. It is what you do with what happens to you.

– Aldous Huxley

S H A P E

Most of the experiences of your life are beyond your control. Yet the Bible says that God uses them to contribute to your SHAPE. Your family experiences, education experiences, vocational experiences, spiritual experiences and painful experiences are stirred together in the pot of life and make up your serving stew. The experiences that you have resented or regretted most of your life, those that you might want to hide or forget, God wants to use to help others. The Bible says that He comforts us in all our troubles so that we can comfort others (II Corinthians 1:4).

A great example of how God uses near calamity to push us forward is the act of walking. When we're walking, we're always in the process of literally falling down. When we move our body forward, we are actually "tripping." But we have learned to move quickly, and so we are "falling" into our next step. If we don't move in a quick and coordinated manner we will fall on our face. In life, as in walking, we lose our balance. But if we respond quickly and correctly, we actually move ourselves forward.

If you hope to maximize the painful experiences of your life, you must be willing to share them. God never wastes an experience, and there is no need for you to be ashamed of them. This is the meaning of Romans 8:28 when it reminds us, "We know that in all things God works for the good of those who love Him, who have been called according to His purpose."

We all have an interesting variety of experiences. You have good and bad experiences gained through your vocation, through spiritual or ministry experiences, or through family, health and social experiences. God uses them all and wants us to honestly admit our faults, failures, fears and fumbles. Why waste your pain? Let it be another's gain.

Joseph had painful experiences with his family that led to slavery in Egypt. It seemed that everything went wrong in his life for 40 years. His life trajectory was a rapid downhill descent. When things began to turn around, he was thrown into jail for a rape he didn't commit and for which he was falsely accused.

Later in his life, things got better. He was raised to second in command in Egypt during a severe famine in which he saved not only that nation but Israel as well. When he was confronted with the brothers who had sold him into slavery he said, "You intended to harm me but God intended it for good."[1]

Even if people have tried to harm you in the past, God can still use it for good. There are lessons to be learned. An unexamined life-experience is worthless. Go back and think through your experiences. What was fulfilling and what wasn't, and what did you learn from both types of experiences? See if you can find life experience patterns. Are there responses that brought better outcomes and opportunities? How could you repeat those in the future? God can use your life experiences to model for, motivate and minister to others.

Don't be surprised if you feel as though all your experiences are not currently useful. Some of them may not be necessary for the next part of your journey. They are lessons learned and are over with. Trying to carry too much baggage may slow you down. Surrender it to God, learn what you can, and leave what you must.

Every year our extended family takes a vacation to the Jersey shore. This tradition goes back to the days of my childhood some 50 years ago. As you can imagine, in all that time we've accumulated some amazing memories. One year my sister was following us in her van with a luggage carrier on top. About halfway down, on the open freeway, she discovered that the carrier was not properly latched and the force from our increasing speed blew the top open. Her family's clothing was all over the highway. We laughed, she cried, and we collected what we could. Of course we could not find everything. There were some items in her wardrobe that had to be counted as a loss.

I am still amused as I imagine other people driving down the highway, seeing her clothing and saying, "Hey, medium-size blouse? I can use that. Size nine sneakers? Sure!"

We're all carrying baggage through life. When the winds blow strong, it may lift off to places unknown. Let it go. It's not destined for this leg of the journey. Through trauma and drama we may have to leave some things by the side of the road. But we learn some lessons and have the freedom to begin again. And don't stop to pick up someone else's baggage. It's not made for you and it won't fit. I am amazed at how many people, with enough difficulties of their own, are willing to pick up someone else's hurt, pain, resentment or bitterness.

For two decades we had family portraits hung on our wall lining the stairway. Each year, at approximately the same time, we would have a picture taken of our family. Watching our three kids change and grow from year to year was a constant source of delight and discussion.

Imagine the stairway of your life. What life experiences would mark each year and, as you ascend the steps, how have these experiences contributed to the person you've become?

Remember, God is crafting a painting of your life, and as He does, He uses all the colors – the dark, painful and difficult ones as well as the bright, delightful, encouraging ones – to complete your portrait. He uses everything in your life for His purpose. Your achievements and experiences become steps in the process of climbing to a fuller understanding of God's ministry plan for you. Keep looking up. Reach higher. If Michelangelo had painted the floor instead of the ceiling of the Sistine Chapel, it would surely be rubbed out by now!

> Do not be afraid to trust God utterly.
> As you go down the long corridor you may find that He has preceded you, and locked many doors which you would fain have entered; but be sure that beyond these there is one that He has left unlocked. Open it and enter, and you will find yourself face to face with a bend of the river of opportunity, broader and deeper than anything you had dared to imagine in your sunniest dreams. Launch forth on it; it conducts to the open sea.[2]
> – F. B. Meyer

REFLECTION

1. Think about two or three of your major achievements. What do they say about who you are?
2. Give an example of how God used apparent failure to bring good things into your life.
3. As you review your life, what experience patterns (see above) can you uncover?
4. Give an example of an experience that you think is unusable to God. Ask a trusted friend how he or she sees it.
5. Read II Corinthians 12:9. What assurance does this verse give those who feel that their weaknesses may disqualify them from service?

CHAPTER 17

TAKE INVENTORY

Congratulations! Today's your day.
You're off to Great Places! You're off and away!
You're on your own. And you know what you know.
And YOU are the guy who'll decide where to go.
— Dr. Seuss

Now that we've looked at the elements of our SHAPE we need to ask the all-important question: "Are we in SHAPE or out of it?" If we're in SHAPE there is focus to our efforts because we know what we're supposed to do. We experience fulfillment because we're doing what lines up with our Divine Design, and we experience fruitfulness because when we do what God made us to do, we get good at it and see results. Passion drives perfection. If we don't care about what we're doing, it's unlikely we'll be good at it.

On the other hand, if we're out of SHAPE, we're likely to feel frustration in our mind, fatigue in our heart and fear in our life because we'll have doubts about our self-worth and meaning.

Anyone who gets anywhere has to begin somewhere. Unfortunately, we seldom accurately assess where we are and what we have along for the journey. David had a sling. Moses had a rod. Aaron had a staff. What do you have? Or can you only think of what you lack? You don't need more strength or more ability or greater opportunities. You need to use what you have.

If we use what we've been given we'll find that more of it will come to us. The challenge with discovering our Divine Design is that we often want to get a great big start. But everything big starts with something small.

In Zechariah 4:10 (TLB), the prophet wrote, "Do not despise the small beginning, for the eyes of the Lord rejoice to see the work begin." Every journey begins with just one step. If it is a step of faith, God will honor it.

Enlargement comes from centrifugal force. Something must be at the center, and for Christians, that is God. He is the source of our growth and enlargement.

In the early part of any journey you have the opportunity to learn more about the path, to grow in wisdom, and to develop faith for the challenges ahead. You may still protest, "But I have so many obstacles!" Remember that it is God's plan that you recognize your needs so that you will turn to Him for help. We are all damaged and in need of repair. That is why God sent Jesus Christ, the Master Builder, not just to put up a new façade, but to reconstruct us.

In Romans 11:29 (NIV) Paul says, "God's gifts and His call are irrevocable." God never removes His gifts and His presence from our life. Even if you haven't discovered your gifting – or you're running from it, or you feel like you've abused it – it's still there! God's gifts are never on loan. They are deposits that are never exhausted, and the more we draw from them, the greater they become.

Psalm 33:13-15 (NKJV) states, "The Lord looks from heaven; He sees [humanity]. From the place of His dwelling He looks on all the inhabitants of the earth; He fashions their hearts individually; He considers all their works." You are a brand new idea from the mind of God. You aren't a backup copy or a designer knockoff. There's no replica of you in all of history, nor will there ever be one of you in the future. You are custom designed and tailor made. Isaiah 43:7 says God personally formed and made each one of us. If you don't know who you are, no one else will either.

There are no unimportant parts to be played. If you play an oboe in God's orchestra, then your notes are required in the song called Living. According to Romans 12:5 (MES), when you do what you do best and give God credit for it, you become a "marvelously functioning part in Christ's body."

In one early visit to a family movie, our young children were intrigued by the empty theater. No previews were running, but there was a spotlight on the stage in front of the seats. In whispers they hatched a plan and before we knew it they had rushed to the front of the auditorium – all three of them dancing around in front of the screen. When we asked what they were doing they said, "We're pretending to be movie stars." Trust me, no one confused them with the actors in a film. When God watches a movie of your life, He doesn't get you confused with anyone else. In Romans 12:5 (MES) Paul writes, "Let's just go ahead and be what we were made to be, without . . . comparing ourselves with each other or trying to be something we aren't."

When our first child was born he looked like E.T. He was wrinkly, toothless and bald. I wanted to send him back because I was pretty sure he wasn't done yet. Never having had children, I didn't realize that there is an unwritten rule that when your relatives and friends see the baby, they have to tell you who he looks like. Imagine my surprise when all the in-laws said, "He looks just like you!" As children we pick up and give labels along the way. "She's uncoordinated, he's just a 'C' student, she's just a plain Jane." Before they know it, these children grow up believing things that are said about them, accepting the label they've been given.

In I Timothy 4:12 (NIV) Paul said, "Don't let anyone look down on you because you are young." We might add:

> "Or because you're poor.
> Or because you're uneducated.
> Or because you're physically challenged.
> Or because you're born a certain race.
> Or because you were unplanned.
> Or because of a mistake in your past."

God's definition of you is the only one that matters, and when you were born He gave you an assignment. Don't give up on life until you've fulfilled it.

In Galatians 6:4-5 (MES), the apostle Paul gave great advice to his friends in Galatia:

> Live creatively, friends . . . Make a careful exploration of who you are and the work you have been given, and then sink yourself into that. Don't be impressed with yourself. Don't compare yourself with others. Each of you must take responsibility for doing the creative best you can with your own life.

Take STOCK . . .

Start small
Trust God for the future
Open yourself to new possibilities
Concentrate on what you've been given, not what you lack
Know who you are and who you're not

What's turning up in your inventory? Take it off the shelf and put it to use for God's purposes.

REFLECTION

1. Take a moment and jot down your top five strengths. Now do the same for your top five weaknesses. Which list took less time to make? Do you think there is a reason for this?
2. Why do you think we become so intolerant of the "small things" in our lives? Can you give some examples of God using small things in the Bible?
3. As you look at your life right now, what small things do you think might have great potential?
4. Can you identify an early life challenge that was labeled an impairment but now looking back you see brought you or God great benefit?
5. Read II Timothy 1:9. How does this verse make comparison of ourselves to others irrelevant?

CHAPTER 18

NOW PUT IT ALL TOGETHER

Most people live in a very restricted circle of their potential being. We all have reservoirs of energy and genius to draw upon of which we do not dream.
—William James

According to Francis Hutcheson, "Wisdom denotes the pursuit of the best ends by the best means." It doesn't matter what others think of you, but it does matter what you think of yourself. God deserves your best. He expects you to make the most of what you've been given. An old Danish proverb states, "What you are is God's gift to you; what you do with yourself is your gift to God."

A helpful step in discovering your Divine Design is to think about your own personal life STORY. Five points will help you put it together:

Strengths – Where are your strengths? Max Lucado states that when God sets you on your journey He didn't give you a knapsack, but a knack sack. These knacks bring results.[1] You may have a knack for bills or budgeting, for planning or proposing, for caring or sharing, for repairing or creating, for organizing or analyzing. My wife has a knack for bringing order to things, my youngest daughter for languages, my son for coaching, my oldest daughter for counseling. I have a knack for refining. Put us all in the same room and you get chaos or creativity – depending on your perspective. (And that's just one household!) Romans 12:6 (NLT) states, "God has given each of us the ability to do certain things well." Think about the things that you can do without much effort. What are the things that you do and wonder why others can't do? These are probably your strengths.

Temperament – Your strengths are usually expressed in a certain way, toward a specific group of people. You are either out front or behind the scenes. You like to work with things or you like to work with people. You leap high to get the big picture or kneel low to sort details. You like the familiarity of repetitive work or you constantly create new things. It's all good for God. Listen to the way He describes a builder by the name of Bezalel in Exodus 31:3-5 (NLT): "I have filled him with the Spirit of God, giving him great wisdom, intelligence, and skill in all kinds of crafts. He is able to create beautiful objects from gold, silver and bronze. He is skilled in cutting and setting gemstones and in carving wood. Yes, he is a master at every craft." God is bragging on one of his kids. Can you sense His pleasure? His delight matches what I feel when I get out pictures of my granddaughter. I say, "Look at her when she does that – she's really good at this." What is your focus or fascination? Whatever it is, when you do it to the best of your ability, God loves to watch you do it and He will help you.

Opportunities – No one can do what you can do, in a way that you can do it, in the situation where you find yourself. You have been born at a particular place and time and you therefore hold the key to specific possibilities. The opportunities that you see are a direct result of your internal wiring. That is why, when you are burdened by a need, you cannot assume someone else will do it. If you perceive it, then you are very likely the one God has chosen to meet it. Think of your talents, gifts, skills and experience. List your friends, colleagues, contacts and coworkers. Consider the ideas that you have for a product or service or business and develop a plan.

Relationships – When you've had your greatest moments of satisfaction or success, how were people involved? Are you stimulated by groups or by working alone? Some assignments don't require a crowd for success. Some people have to lead a group of others, some need to be followers. It is important to examine your relational pattern. If you like to motivate others but spend the majority of your time in front of a computer screen, your life may not be as fulfilling as it could be.

Yield – As you examine your life STORY you will no doubt find those peaks where it seemed like everything came together and resulted in unexpected success. What was your role at those times? How did you contribute to the results? As you look back on your life, what has brought the greatest rewards? It may be wise to invest yourself there.

Combining the various elements of your STORY may be a way to get a clearer look at your Divine Design. Your STORY is a glimpse of your unique fingerprint. Everyone loves something. If we ignore our passions we waste the great potential God has placed within us. It's been said that most winners are just ex-losers who got passionate. Use your STORY to help springboard yourself into the future, putting the many pieces of your puzzle together.

E. Paul Hovey said, "A blind man's world is bounded by the limits of his touch; an ignorant man's world by the limits of his knowledge; a great man's world by the limits of his vision." We limit our potential because we only have vision for one part of our STORY. Imagine how hard it would be to make sense of a newspaper article if you were only fed a few random sentences. How much would you admire a painting if it only had one color? Have you ever gone to a carnival or fair and become an instant artist? In a cylinder is a piece of paper on which you squirt a variety of paint colors. Then you turn a switch and the cylinder spins, creating your own unique masterpiece. Many people apply only one color to their life story. They examine only their strengths or opportunities or relationships without realizing the beauty of blending them all together.

You must work to learn as much about yourself as you can. Try to fill in the colors of your STORY. Perhaps by looking back, you will be able to see farther ahead. Perch yourself high on the peak of a few of your successes and scan the horizon. What do you see? How does it help you understand more about your place in the world?

But don't stand on that height for too long. You must come back down or you may find yourself bleached and parched in the intensity of the blistering rays of the sun. There is a balance between analysis and activity. We won't learn all we need to know by observation – we must get back on the playing field.

Vince Lombardi would add, "I firmly believe that any man's finest hour – his greatest fulfillment to all he holds dear – is that moment when he has worked his heart out in a good cause and lies exhausted on the field of battle – victorious."

Learn all you can about yourself and then use that knowledge to serve others by helping them discover their design.

REFLECTION

1. Take a moment to write out the highlights of your own life STORY.

2. How is this story different from that of other members of your immediate family who experienced many of the same things in life that you did?

3. What makes this story different from that of those in the larger network of your family and friends?

4. How might God use these uniquenesses for His purposes and glory?

5. Sociologists tell us our self-esteem is shaped by what we believe the most important people in our lives think about us. What relevance does I Thessalonians 1:4 lend to that discussion, especially when you are tempted to reject parts of your STORY?

CHAPTER 19

POTHOLES AND ROADBLOCKS

Listen to your life. See it for the fathomless mystery it is, in the boredom and pain of it no less than in the excitement and gladness: Touch, taste, smell your way to the holy and hidden heart of it because in the last analysis all moments are key moments, and life itself is grace.
— Frederick Buechner

When was your last wobbly ride? I try to give thought to my physical conditioning. In my 30s I played tennis (until I injured my elbow). In my 40s I turned to jogging (until I developed shin splints). Now in my 50s I've turned to biking (until I crash?). One of the things I've learned is that you can't ride very far with a loose spoke. One bad spoke can stress the others until they all begin to loosen, and your whole ride will become unstable, or worse. Each spoke matters, and when one is not fixed firmly in its proper place, the balance and the integrity of the wheel is compromised. You will be left stranded by the roadside.

You've seen it happen, haven't you – where people streak off for a win in life? They are way out ahead of you and then they hit a pothole and a spoke loosens, and when you come across them they are a roadside casualty.

I've found there are five extremely important arenas, or "spokes," to pay attention to in life. Life has its elements. It is a whole with many parts. You can't live out of one compartment. Take an objective look at the different aspects of your life and see how the parts relate to each other as well as to the whole:

- Personal – this is the arena that contains your SHAPE and life STORY
- Family – this arena includes parents, spouse, children and influential extended family members
- Church – this arena includes persons in opportunities to serve others within the body of Christ
- Vocation – this is the arena of work or career
- Community – this is the arena where a person gives back to society at large through volunteer service in his or her own neighborhood or region

Without leading a balanced life in each of these five areas, you will not be effective in developing your Divine Design. Failure in any one of these areas can become a roadblock in the path of your promise.

Each domain affects all the others. For example, if a person experiences a failure in family life, it will certainly have an effect on his vocation. If a person is not growing personally, it will be difficult for her to find effective ministry or community influence.

While all the areas are not necessarily equal in terms of time allocation, each is a necessary part of the whole. The center hub from which all the spokes radiate is Jesus Christ. The Bible says in II Corinthians 5:14 (MES), "Christ's love has the first and last word in everything we do. Our firm decision is to work from this focused center."

Certainly it is impossible to be balanced perfectly. But the first step toward going somewhere significant is deciding that you are not going to stay where you are. There's an old Chinese proverb that states: "Man stand for long time with mouth open before roast duck fly in." The farmers in our area have their own version. "You have to sit a very long time in an open field with your milk pail before a cow backs up to you." The point is, we have to stay engaged with life. We don't sit down and give up. We never arrive. Like the apostle Paul, we're constantly pressing toward that higher calling in Christ Jesus (Philippians 3:12).

Of course it's up to you. You get to make the decisions. But if you don't decide what's important in your life, someone else is likely to decide for you. Your destiny is not a matter of chance; it's a matter of choice. Without deciding what you are committing yourself to, you stand in the middle of the road. That is a very dangerous location because you can get knocked down by traffic coming from both directions. Joshua Chamberlain understood the power that lies in the deciding when he wrote from the battle of Gettysburg:

> We know not of the future, and cannot plan for it much. But we can hold our spirits and our bodies so pure and high, we may cherish such thoughts and such ideals, and dream such dreams of lofty purpose, that we can determine and know what manner of men we will be whenever and wherever the hour strikes that calls to noble action . . . No man becomes suddenly different from his habit and cherished thought.

It is your decisions that help you navigate the hairpin turns and high-speed merges that occur on life's highway. The road is dangerous, filled with potholes and roadblocks. You certainly don't want to be caught in those dangerous situations with equipment that can't sustain you. Check your balance. Examine the spokes of your life. Then make a quality decision to bring things into better alignment so you will be able to navigate any obstacles to your Divine Design.

REFLECTION

1. Why do you think so many gifted people seem to self-destruct?
2. As you personally examine the five spokes of life listed above, which of yours do you think is strongest right now? Which is weakest? Ask a trusted friend to verify your findings.
3. Can you think of an example of someone whose weakened life-spoke led to a crash? Could you see it coming? Do you think the person could? How could you tell?
4. Give an example of how easy it is for people to decide what's most important for you. How did you handle their decisions about you?
5. Deciding to keep life in balance is hard. Every choice involves a risk. How did David find comfort for the risks he was experiencing in Psalm 32:7?

CHAPTER 20

ME, MYSELF AND WHY

God doesn't play dice.
— Albert Einstein

Who is better qualified to be you than you? We spent many chapters reinforcing the idea that each person has been given specific gifts, passion, talents, personality and strengths. As incredible as it sounds, most people actually spend their entire lives trying to change the way they were made. Christians have a tremendous advantage in life when they understand that the way we were made pleases God. If God is pleased, shouldn't we be, too?

Then why are so many people jealous of the way others were made? Why do we try to copy others and, by doing so, overlook our own true talents and abilities? In Romans 12 the Bible makes it clear that if you are a teacher you should teach. If you enjoy serving, then do so. If you are a musician, make music. As honest Abe said, "Whatever you are, be a good one."

Why are we so scared of originality? A number of years ago, a university was accused of plagiarism (taking the writings of someone else and passing them off as one's own). What was unusual was that the school had plagiarized the section on plagiarism from another university's handbook. A news report stated, "A graduate student of one school, who was considering a teaching assistant's job at the other, was reading the school handbook when he noted that the section warning students against plagiarism was identical to the caution in the handbook of the other university." Even those who know better tend to copy. Eric Hoffer said: "When people are free to do as they please, they usually imitate each other."[1]

You must have a solid grip on your Divine Design. The world is doing its best to reshape you into everybody else. William Matthews said, "One well-cultivated talent, deepened and enlarged, is worth a hundred shallow faculties."

We were created and designed to fulfill God's purpose and represent His interests on earth. He is the creator who molds and shapes us.[2] And His shaping does not reflect just our outer form. Psalm 139 reads:

> . . . you shaped me first inside, then out; you formed me
> in my mother's womb.
> Body and soul, I am marvelously made!
> You know me inside and out.
> You know every bone in my body;
> you know exactly how I was made, bit by bit,
> and how I was sculpted from nothing into something.[3]

God supervises every aspect of the creative process, the spiritual as well as the physical.

This design theology can be seen in the New Testament as well. Paul draws an analogy between the body of Christ (believers who make up the Church) and the human body. Just as God's design is evident in the human body, so it is in His spiritual body. Spiritual gifts in the church reflect this principle of design.

God is the author of our design and though He has made each of us different, we are all needed to accomplish His purpose. In a world that seems fixed on helping us discover what's wrong with us, it is important to know what is right with us. Our Divine Design gives us this information. You may love what someone else loathes. Each of us is wired differently, so what makes another feel weak may actually make you feel strong. Understanding our differences helps us capitalize on them.

Your capabilities make you a "10" somewhere. But you have to believe it. As Ralph Hodgson says, "Some things have got to be believed to be seen." In other words, we act consistent with what we believe. Believe you are "gifted" and you will exercise your gifts. The discovery of your Divine Design helps you to determine precisely where you should apply your energies for the greatest return.

In addition, your Divine Design does not change with age, marital status, education or location. While it is true that the application of your design may differ as you grow older or change life circumstance, your basic orientation toward life remains constant. This means that an investment in understanding the way that you are made will bring rewards throughout your lifetime.

Understanding our Divine Design is also a great antidote to poor self-esteem. The growing number of emotional and spiritual self-help books indicates that a negative attitude toward oneself is becoming epidemic. The

Bible, on the other hand, teaches us that we should love ourselves (Matthew 19:19).

Knowing and liking yourself will naturally lead to you being your best self. You will not try to pretend or be boastful of your gifts, because you know they are God-given. As you become convinced of the wonder and beauty of your design you will be able to accept yourself as God accepts you and, as a result, be able to demonstrate humility and show support to other people.

Because you have strengths where others are weak and vice versa, you will notice your need for others. The fact that we are not given all the gifts is a reminder to us of our need for others. The fact is, we are better together. No one has every gift or strength. Romans 15:17 (NIV) states that we are to "accept one another, then, just as Christ accepted us, in order to bring praise to God." We are to do life together. We can then make the maximum use of our gifts in a way that benefits the whole. Zig Ziglar states, "You'll always have everything you want in life, if you'll help enough other people get what they want." While your Divine Design starts with you, it certainly doesn't end there.

A properly understood design gives us not just me and myself, but why.

REFLECTION

1. What would your "perfect life" look like? If you were to complete the sentence "I'm finally doing what I've always dreamed of doing, which is . . ." what would it include?

2. Think through the metaphor of God as the "Potter" and you as the "clay." What five lessons about that idea can you draw? (For example, "I shouldn't jump off the wheel before the Potter is finished.")

3. Think of Paul's analogy comparing the human body with the body of Christ. What part of the human body are you most like?

4. Why do you think it's so hard for Christians to love themselves? What part of your design is hardest for you to accept?

5. Read Romans 15:7. Describe how a fuller understanding of your Divine Design will impact others. Can you give an example?

CHAPTER 21

YOUR DIVINE DESIGN AND GOD'S WILL

The man without a purpose is like a ship without a rudder — a waif, a nothing, a no man.
— Thomas Carlyle

Long before your conception, you were conceived in the mind of God. You were first an idea of His. It is not by accident that you stand on the earth at this point in time among a constellation of acquaintances, friends and relatives with a certain mix of gifts, passion and personality. You are alive because God wanted you. The Bible says in Psalm 138:8 (NIV), "The Lord will fulfill His purpose for me."

God even went so far in demonstrating His care for you to send His Son to die on the cross and rescue you from self-destruction. In a 1990 television documentary on the U.S. Civil War, a letter was read that was written by a soldier killed in the battle of Bull Run. Sullivan Ballou realized the end was near so he wrote a touching letter to his wife. It said, "If I do not return, my dear Sarah, never forget how much I loved you, nor that when my last breath escapes me on the battlefield, it will whisper your name."[1]

When Christ's last breath escaped Him on the cross, it was whispering your name. That's how important you are. But He didn't just die for you. He freed you from your selfish tendencies so you could follow His pattern of living for others.

God left no detail of your life to chance. He planned it all for His purpose. Nothing in your life is random or accidental.

Why would God go to all the trouble? The Bible says it was because of His love. He created each person as a special object of His love. And He loved you in the hope that you would love Him back.

Perhaps that is why, whenever a handful of Christians get together, it is just a matter of time until someone brings up the subject of the will of God. If God loves us, and created us for a purpose, how do we follow His plan? How do we know whom to marry, where to live, what vocation to pursue or how much to pay for a car or a home? Is God really interested in that level of detail? In a country where there are 50,000 ways to make a living, what does God want you to choose for a career? Those are fair questions.

Even though you have a Divine Design, it's important to realize that God's will for your life is not fixed. If God has a definite plan, a blueprint, a unique specification for our lives, does that mean that when we make a mistake in life, God has to throw out the plan and start over? No, our choices do not surprise God. His plan was formed with full knowledge of our choices. God's will for your life encompasses your failures and shortcomings. You haven't missed the boat. You aren't disqualified. You haven't lost the race. I often tell people that God's will is much more about the "what" than the "where, when and how." When deciding between two jobs, it's not that one is God's will and the other is not (unless your work involves some kind of illegal or harmful activity). The issue is, will you be God's representative at either one? And which most needs the influence of a loving and caring Heavenly Father? So often we twist the issue of God's will and make it about us rather than Him. Shall I take the job with the reserved parking spot and six weeks of vacation or the one that pays $10,000 more?

God leaves many of the decisions surrounding His will up to us, and that's why it is so important for us to understand our Divine Design. As we understand more about the way in which we're made, we will be better positioned to choose the roles in which we can serve God best.

One word that separates Christianity from other religions is *serving*. We discover our Divine Design so that we can be better servants of God. I Peter 4:10 (NLT) states, "God has given each of you a gift from His great variety of spiritual gifts. Use them well to serve one another." Ultimately the will of God is whatever you desire – if you are following Him, allowing Him to fill you, submitting to Him and serving Him. Psalm 37:4 (TLB) says: "Be delighted with the Lord. Then He will give you all your heart's desires."

Remember that as you make decisions about the will of God, they can never be contrary to the Word of God. When the Bible forbids premarital sex, it makes no sense to justify living together with a member of the opposite sex by saying, "We really love each other so it must be God's will." Michelangelo said, "The greater danger for most of us is not that our aim is too high and we miss it, but that it is too low and we reach it."

The Bible makes clear that:

- The will of God for your life is good
- The will of God includes your salvation
- The will of God is revealed to you and not others
- The will of God is not contrary to His Word
- The will of God is for you to express your Divine Design

Where to go to school? Where to live? What church to attend? What job to select? Whatever you want. If you are living a life of Christian commitment, then your desire will be God's will for you because God establishes those desires in your heart. He will use your innermost feelings and your Divine Design to help direct your path.

My father would much rather work with his hands than study a book, so when I was in grade school he wasn't so interested in how I did in my "subjects." The mark he cared most about on my report card was the one next to the line that read "conduct." While getting the right answer was good, he thought what was more important was my attitude and respect for others. To him it wasn't so much about *what* I did as it was about *how* I did it. You may find the same to be true when discerning God's will for your life.

REFLECTION

1. Do you think there is a relationship between God's will and the way that you were designed? Explain.
2. What clues about God's will do you detect by looking at the way you were made?
3. Do you think it's possible to pursue the details of God's will in a way that is unproductive? If so, how?
4. Is it easier to uncover insights about your Divine Design through education or service? Give an example.
5. Read I Corinthians 13:5. Explain why love, as it is defined here, helps us pursue God's way rather than our own.

CHAPTER 22

EXTREME MAKEOVERS OF THE MIND

Your thought is the parent that gives birth to all things.
— Neale Donald Walsch

In *Anatomy of the Spirit*, Caroline Myss states: "Managing the power of choice, with all its creative and spiritual implications, is the essence of human experience . . . Choice is the process of creation itself." So how do we make choices about what we most want to be, do, have and contribute?

At some point we must give attention to our mental processes. Dr. Robert H. Schuller once stated, "The only place your dream becomes impossible is in your own thinking." You must consider the possibility that what is stopping you is what you believe – that in effect you are stopping yourself. All of us have a belief window through which we see the world. On our belief window are those things that we believe to be true about the patterns of the world, ourselves, and others. They might be as obvious as "When I drop this glass it will fall to the ground" to something as arguable as "All men are pigs." Our beliefs might be based on scientific evidence and testing and might reflect things as they really are. On the other hand, we might have beliefs that are twisted from reality, such as "No one is trustworthy." Faith may be required for some beliefs, such as "In spite of my difficult circumstances, I know God is still in control."

Here's the point: No matter what it is we believe to be true, we will act as though it is true. In Proverbs 23:7 (NKJV) Solomon says, "For as [a man] thinks in his heart, so is he." Our focus determines our outcomes. Romans 12:2 (NEV) states, "Adapt yourselves no longer to the pattern of this present world, but let your minds be remade and your whole nature transformed."

If you hold the belief that failure is bad or that God is mad at you or that you'll never amount to anything, chances are you will align your actions with those beliefs. The things that we "believe" tend to determine our future. If we hope to produce positive behavior, we must hold beliefs that are absolutely correct. Incorrect beliefs will produce negative, self-defeating behavior. Take gossiping for example. This negative behavior usually springs from a need to feel important and desire to be appreciated and loved. Much gossiping occurs to pull other people down so that we feel more important. The "belief" that we have the right to judge other people will result in a host of enemies and a poor reputation. On the other hand, if we hold the belief that we are to accept and love others, then a whole different set of behaviors emerges.

The roughly three pounds of tissue that compose the human brain is interlaced by more than 100 billion neurons, each reaching out with some 1,000 "fingers" to connect with other neurons. That means that the brain contains roughly 100 trillion connections – more than the number of galaxies in the known universe.[1] It is out of this mental powerhouse that you assess your world to gain yourself the right beliefs that will keep you from getting lost in the negative messages that surround you. Reviewing your understanding of your design a hundred times a day will cause your brain to make thousands and millions of connections far beneath the level of your consciousness. Initially, the changing of these neuroconnections will alter your behavior. But ultimately you'll do 90 percent to 99 percent of what you do without being conscious that your mind has connected positively to your beliefs.

While we do have a free will, we are automatically anchored to a multitude of stimuli that we don't acknowledge or even recognize. These stimuli are catalysts that produce responses of mood and feelings, action and thought. By purposely selecting the right anchors for your belief system you will find yourself making increased progress toward the full benefit of your Divine Design. What are the right anchors?

Here are some:

- God loves you and has a wonderful plan for your life
- Life goes better when you follow the wisdom of God found in the Bible
- God wants you to share His love with others
- God wants you to practice a lifestyle of integrity, diligence and service . . . you get the idea

The beliefs of your mind can play tricks on you. They can keep you from setting challenging goals in faith and lull you into playing it safe. Listen to the words of Sir Francis Drake:

Disturb us, Lord, when we are too well pleased with ourselves. When our dreams have come true because we dreamed too little. When we arrive safely because we have sailed too close to the shore. Disturb us, Lord.[2]

There's another aspect of our mind that we need to consider besides our belief system. It is what Tom Paterson calls our built-in "thinking wavelength." It is our way of organizing the world, tolerating change and juggling all the variables.[3] Thinking wavelength takes place on a spectrum of concrete to abstract . . . from doers on the one hand to theorists on the other. See if you can identify yourself on the following continuum:

- Grinders – These are detail-minded doers. Grinders like to plow through the work one step at a time and are averse to change.
- Minders – These "mind the store" types can solve routine problems and can often keep a small group focused and on task.
- Keepers – Keepers tend to be more strategic and administrative. They can handle variables, are organized and usually work well with people.
- Finders – Finders are entrepreneurs. They don't like paperwork and relish change. They are great at seizing opportunities.
- Theorists – Theorists are bright, articulate and persuasive. They take a long time to bring anything to closure. They have a high tolerance for ambiguity and would rather postulate than execute. They love the big picture.

The important thing to remember here is that our thinking wavelength is a part of our Divine Design. It is not likely to change much over the course of our lifetime. It is wise to find opportunities for work and service to capitalize on our particular mental focus. It may require an extreme makeover of the mind.

REFLECTION

1. Can you think of an example of when your belief system about something changed? (It could be as simple as "I don't like anything

with seeds" to something more serious, like "Homeless people are lazy.") What was the impact of your new belief?

2. Describe a change you've made in a religious belief. How has it affected your actions?

3. What "anchors" for your beliefs will keep you from getting "off track"?

4. In which category do you place yourself – Grinders, Minders, Keepers, Finders or Theorists? Give an example. Of the remaining options, who do you need most? Why?

5. Read II Corinthians 10:5. How do we capture "thoughts" and subject them to our Divine Design? Give an example of a thought that got away from you this week.

CHAPTER 23

THE IMPORTANCE OF PAUSE, PRAYER AND REFLECTION

Hurry is not of the devil; it is the devil.
— Psychiatrist C. G. Jung

If you've gotten this far in your reading then you must understand that a relationship with God is required for you to understand your Divine Design. (It is a DIVINE design after all.) Though you may be a moral, decent, law-abiding person, you may not be enjoying God's best if you lack a relationship with your Designer. While you may know plenty of successful people who don't pay much attention to their spiritual life, that is not God's plan for you (or for them, but they don't know it yet). You and I were made by God, for God. He created us to know and love Him. In Acts 17:28 (NKJV) Paul says, "In Him we live and move and have our being." Just like lungs need oxygen, just like fish need water, just like e-mail needs an electronic device, we need God. From beginning to end the Bible is a story of God pursuing humankind and humankind pursuing God. But something has gotten in the way. God calls the problem sin, and it has hindered our relationship with Him ever since Adam and Eve ate the forbidden fruit.

Whether we want to admit it or not, we will never be fulfilled or fruitful until we bring our need for love and acceptance to God and ask Him to meet it. There is no way that you can exist outside a living, growing relationship with the One who made you. You can experience God's comfort, healing and forgiveness. Perhaps up to this point you've trusted only yourself and our study together has shown that you need outside help. Simply transfer responsibility of your life to God's capable hands. Admit how selfish and arrogant it is to try to manage life as though you were in control of the universe. Accept the fact that God wants to lead your life and has created you with a plan and purpose. Receive His forgiveness and invite Him into your life. Not only will He forgive and empower you, but He will provide you with an eternal home in heaven.

If you've already taken this step, it's important for you to realize that there is no way you can uncover your Divine Design without stepping off life's train long enough to decide if it's heading where you want to go. The frenzy of life, filled with its calendar of tasks and demands, often keeps us from slowing down. Jesus says in Mark 6:31 (MES), "Come off by yourselves; let's take a break and get a little rest." The context for this verse is Jesus entering into the public arena. Thrilled masses, just-healed believers, and thousands of others were following Him. So does Jesus give His "I Have a Dream" speech, organize triage for the sick and needy or solicit media moguls for a public relations campaign? No. He baffled his pundits by slipping away to a deserted place. What was His point? He needed time for pause, for prayer, for reflection. If Jesus needed that, so do you.

Just like in Jesus' case, the people you relate to won't consult your strengths or know your STORY. They won't mind advising you about where you should work, whom you should marry or what course of study you should pursue.

The chief way to get clarity about your Divine Design is to set time to be alone. But you can be alone and still not be focused. I will never forget my visit to Paris in the spring of 1998. Though it was nearly 10 years ago, on a damp day I still feel the pain in my shoulders. Sally and I had gone to visit our son, who was doing a spring semester of his college education in Europe. After a visit to the Palace of Versailles, we had a train to catch for our next city. Gridlock in the streets had stopped all traffic so we had to cover the two miles to the train station by foot, carrying several hundred pounds of luggage between us. (I never go anywhere without my books. And books are heavy!) The gentleman in charge of our tour had only a light souvenir bag to carry and was moving briskly. Up and down steps, around construction sites, adrenaline pumping through our veins, we moved as fast as possible, stepping onto the train just as the doors closed. We stumbled to our seats and collapsed. It was then that the full force of our exertion overtook us. Barely able to breathe, unable to drink, it took us nearly an hour to recover. It was an experience our bodies won't let us forget.

The high stress and hectic pace of our daily lives make it very difficult to recover when we go panting through life. The moment we try to meditate, the aches and pains of a burdened journey rise to the surface. We often enter our time to meet God with bodies heading for the next city while our emotions are still attached to our last experience. It's hard to concentrate our thoughts and quietly relax.

Ernie Johnson followed in his father's footsteps as a major league baseball announcer. When asked about the most memorable games he covered,

Ernie reflected back to his days as a nine-year-old Little Leaguer. An opposing batter hit the ball, which bounded over the fence for a ground-rule double. Two outfielders scampered over the barrier to retrieve the ball so the game could continue. Both teams waited and waited and waited for them to return. No one appeared. Concerned coaches jogged into the outfield followed by equally concerned parents. After scaling the fence, they discovered the missing pair. There they were, just a few feet beyond the fence, gloves dropped on the ground, newly recovered ball at their feet, blackberries and smiles on their faces. Sometimes, no matter how important the activity, we just need to take a break!

Christ found the need to escape the noise of the crowd in order to hear the voice of God. He resisted the pull of people trying to sweep Him along in the wake of their agenda. Martin Luther followed his example. He is quoted as saying, "I have so much to do today I need to spend another hour on my knees."

What do you do when you sense there is a disconnect between your design and your duties? Psalm 37:7 (NLT) says, "Be still in the presence of the Lord, and wait patiently for Him to act." The practice of being silent, of praying, of meditating is not an easy one to learn. But it is essential if you want to grow in the ways of your Divine Design.

Leonard Sweet writes of an exhausted father who hurriedly bent down to give his son a quick kiss on the cheek, then walked out of the room feeling utterly spent. The son's question, "Why do you kiss me so fast?" pierced the father's fatigue. Sweet goes on to ask, "Why do we let the most precious moments of life go by so fast? Why do we kiss the best things in life so hurriedly?"[1]

John Ortberg writes, "Again and again, as we pursue spiritual life, we must do battle with hurry. For many of us the great danger is not that we will renounce our faith, it is that we will become so distracted and rushed and preoccupied that we will settle for a mediocre version of it."[2]

Hurry and its routines become enemies of our spiritual development. We must take steps to break its hold on us.

On a visit to Germany my wife and I went to visit the majestic Cologne Cathedral. What we didn't realize was that in this particular year, that area was a major venue for the World Cup Soccer championships. Stepping out of our train into the grand plaza, we were overcome with the chaos and cacophony of tourists who were marching around and shouting for their favorite team. Folks who had come to admire the majestic beauty of this wonderful expression of worship were distracted by people in costumes, bands playing and heads painted to look like soccer balls.

The scene reminded me of the challenge that we all face, how when we have a desire to pull back and see God through prayer or reflection, the distractions of the world – be they a newspaper, an unpaid bill or a list of things to be done – pull us away.

Take a personal retreat with God, time away from the rhythm of life just to be with your Creator. Pick a place far from your routine duties – a park, a stream, a hotel, a beach, the mountains.
Ask yourself the following questions:

- What do I feel good about right now?
- What do I feel bad about right now?
- What's missing from my life?
- What should be eliminated from my life?
- If I could imagine God speaking to me now, what would He say?

Without time for pause, prayer and reflection, we may unknowingly run right past God's plan for our design.

REFLECTION

1. Do other people – especially those who know me best – think I work too much or I am under too much stress?
2. The Bible instructs us to be still and know that God is God (Psalm 46:10). On the surface this looks like a strange declaration. What do you think it means?
3. Think back to your personal times with God since your conversion. Has the frequency and/or quality of those times been increasing or decreasing?
4. In the middle of your next stress attack, do something kind for someone else that was unexpected or undeserved. How might that make you feel?
5. Read Isaiah 64:4. Can you give an example of God acting on your behalf as you were waiting for Him?

CHAPTER 24

THE VALUES MATRIX

We don't see things as they are, we see them as we are.
— Anais Nin

This past spring we had a garage sale. Furniture, clothing, books and tools lined our driveway. We didn't make a lot of money. That didn't surprise us. What did surprise us were the items that sold. Ripped rugs, damaged mirrors and dusty paintings were loaded on the back of pickup trucks and station wagons and hauled away.

Apparently people value things differently. One man's trash is another man's treasure. There's an old business principle that states: "An object's worth is what someone is willing to pay for it." Perhaps there are times in your life when you've thought, *I don't matter. I'm of no account. I'm not valuable.* But when you begin to doubt your worth all you need to do is to remember the price God paid for you – on the cross. I Peter 1:18-19 (TLB) states, "God paid a ransom to save you . . . He paid for you with the precious life-blood of Christ."

It is clear that God places a high value on our lives. He values us. But what do you value? You can't value everything equally. Your Divine Design requires you to assign relative values to your goals and activities. When Benjamin Franklin was 22 years old he came up with his own values plan. He called it "a bold and arduous project of arriving at moral perfection." After considerable thought he came up with 12 virtues that were to be his governing values. They included such things as order, frugality, industry, justice and tranquility. A Quaker friend looked at them and informed Franklin that he forgot an important one: humility![1] Franklin then wrote, as part of his definition for humility, "imitate Jesus." He confessed at the end of his life that while he never attained perfection, he was much better than he would have been if he hadn't identified his values.

Most people don't know what's really most important to them, so they don't recognize it even if it stares them in the face. They are like the manager who sent a memo to his staff that said, "The firings will continue until morale improves!" You need to know your values so you can recognize what is important to you.

One way to understand your values was illustrated to me in a seminar I attended long ago. The presenter discussed the things in life we were willing to carry across our "I beam."[2] In case you are unaware, an I beam is the basic steel beam that's used in construction. It's called an I beam because a cross section of it looks like a capital I. The presenter asked us to imagine an I beam brought to our house. He stands at one end where he places a $100 bill. He then invites us to walk across it and pick up the money. If we do so without falling off, the money is ours. Obviously it's not a very difficult task. The presenter then asked the participants to suppose he were to take the I beam on the back of a truck to Lower Manhattan and place it across the two buildings then known as the World Trade Center towers. He would then place the $100 bill at one end of the beam. The presenter then asked, "Would you be willing to walk across the beam for $100?" (It gets pretty windy up there.) No one in the seminar would agree to do it. He offered to raise the amount to $1,000, $10,000, $100,000 or even $1 million. He then explained that the reason people wouldn't come across the I beam is because they value life more than they value money. He then made a shocking suggestion. He said, "If you have a two-year-old daughter and I'm standing at one end holding her by her arms and telling you that if you don't make your way across the I beam I would drop your daughter, would you come now?" It becomes very clear that there are a few things for which we would cross the I-beam. Suddenly we realize that there are some things that we value more than life itself – our two-year-old daughter might be one of them.

Money has value, safety has value. But our love of a child has an even greater value.

You can see how your values have an impact on your Divine Design. If you were offered another job in another state, for more money, would you take it? In other words, do you value your income more than your friends, family and church in the area? How much money would it take for you to change your mind?

The fact is, different people have different values. Take King David for example. He clued us in to his values in Psalm 27:4 (NIV) when he said, "One thing I ask of the Lord. This is what I seek: That I might dwell in the house of the Lord all the days of my life, and gaze upon the beauty of the Lord and seek Him in His Temple." In other words, David valued intimacy with God. We might guess that his son, Solomon, valued wisdom.[3]

How many of these values show up on your list?

- Loving God with all your heart, mind and strength
- Loving your neighbor as yourself
- Obeying the commandments of God
- Being a great husband, wife, daughter, mother, father
- Honesty
- Humility
- Generosity
- Loyalty
- Purity
- Kindness

If you want to fully experience God's Divine Design, then the things that you value in life must match the things that the Bible calls most valuable. What do you treasure most?

Four young men sit at the bedside of their dying father. The old man, with his last breath, tells them there's a huge treasure buried in the family fields. The sons crowd around him, crying, "Where, where?" But it's too late. The day after the funeral, and for many days to come, the young men go out with their picks and shovels and turn the soil, digging deeply into the ground from one end of each field to the other. They find nothing and, bitterly disappointed, abandon the search. The next season the farm has its best harvest ever.[4]

REFLECTION

1. Sometimes we hear the expression "If I was the only one to save, Christ still would have died." Do you think so? Why or why not?

2. List the things you value in order of importance. Does the importance of these things match the quantities of time you assign to them? Where does there need to be an adjustment?

3. What value of yours has been climbing up your priority list in the last year? Which value has been declining? Is this intentional?

4. What biblical value do you most need to adopt in this stage of your life? What plan will you use to make this change?
5. See Isaiah 43:25. If the value of an object is determined by what one is willing to pay for it, what must your value be to God?

CHAPTER 25

YOUR SWEET SPOT

"For I know the thoughts that I think toward you," says the Lord, "thoughts of peace and not of evil, to give you a future and a hope."
– Jeremiah 29:11 (NKJV)

My first trip to the U.S. Open was to see Andre Agassi bid his farewell to tennis. In one of Agassi's moments of brilliance, the person next to me said, "Andre manages his sweet spot better than anyone else in tennis."

In the world of sports, the "sweet spot" is the place on the racket or club that strikes the ball with maximum effectiveness and minimum resistance. It's one of the reasons that athletes like Barry Bonds, Andre Agassi and Tiger Woods swing so smoothly yet with great range.

Your sweet spot is the place where the various parts of your SHAPE (spiritual gifts, heart, abilities, personality and experiences) intersect with your Kingdom purpose. It manifests when your mind, will and heart are in complete alignment.

We should pay attention when someone identifies our sweet spot. When someone celebrates what we do best, we should pay close attention to what they are affirming. They may be telling us an important truth about how God made us and how we were meant to function.

While teaching on this subject at my church, I donned my tennis attire and brought my tennis racquet and some balls. After each of my main points, I hit a tennis ball in the auditorium. (You might think this is overkill, but my hits did keep the audience awake!) I had two goals. One was not to hurt anyone (including myself) and the other was not to hit the microphone suspended from the ceiling in the middle of the auditorium. I succeeded in one of my two goals. What are the chances of a three-inch ball hitting a three-inch microphone in an auditorium that seats 1,200 people? Pretty small, but I managed it. I learned an important lesson. Focusing on what you want to avoid draws you to it.

Sometimes information may be packaged in such a negative way that we internalize it. For example, suppose your neighbors begin talking about a subject on which you've done a bit of research. As they talk, you share some of the details, and perhaps even correct some of their misinformation. Rather than being identified as a careful researcher, you may be labeled as a know-it-all. Organized people may be classified as perfectionists. Outgoing extroverts may be called drama queens. Technical wizards may be called geeks. Public figures may be called glory hounds. There's a sense of shame attached to these labels, which can actually keep us from doing more of those things that lie in our sweet spot.

Remember that the purpose of your life is to put your God-given gifts and abilities to work for Kingdom impact. These gifts are to be leveraged for good in your arena of service and in your sphere of influence. Finding your sweet spot involves focusing on what you can do, not what you can't. Focusing on the tools you've been given, not those you haven't. Zeroing in on your strengths, not your weaknesses. But your Divine Design involves more than just liking what you do and being gifted at what you do. It also includes succeeding to the point of excellence. When you serve others with excellence within your design's sweet spot, you'll feel little resistance and accomplish more than you ever expected.

The Bible puts it this way:

> God has given each of us the ability to do certain things well. So if God has given you the ability to prophesy, speak out when you have faith that God is speaking through you. If your gift is that of serving others, serve them well. If you are a teacher, do a good job of teaching. If your gift is to encourage others, do it! If you have money, share it generously. If God has given you leadership ability, take the responsibility seriously. And if you have a gift for showing kindness to others, do it gladly. Romans 12:6-8 (NLT)

You'll know that you have hit your sweet spot when your service becomes both effective and effortless at the same time. It's the place where your focus, fruitfulness and fulfillment all come together.

But our service will never become effective without practice. Jim Ryun states that "Motivation is what gets you started, habit is what keeps you going." The discipline of repetitive action is required. Just like with strength training in the gym, the "muscles" we use for service develop when we experience resistance. In "The Rime of the Ancient Mariner," English poet Samuel Taylor Coleridge describes tempests and doldrums at sea. Two lines have become household words:

> Water, water everywhere,
> Nor any drop to drink.

In doldrum latitudes, the wind dies down and the sailing ship remains stationary. Captain and crew are "stuck," with no relief in sight. Eventually, with no wind, their water supply runs out and they face destruction. Life in our sweet spot requires the resistance of the wind. Without it, our lives may remain calm, but we make little progress and eventually die of boredom or complacency.[1]

Far too many people settle for less than God intended. They engage in activities that are too small for their spirit and end up floating in a doldrum. They don't hit the ball at all, let alone connect with their sweet spot. It doesn't have to be that way. We live in an unfinished world so that we can share in the joys and satisfaction of creation. Don't just dream of great accomplishments. Identify your sweet spot and then stay awake and live the dream.

REFLECTION

1. What areas of your life do you feel may fall within your sweet spot? Why do you think so?
2. If your Divine Design were published as a book, what would its title be?
3. In what areas do others seem to appreciate your efforts although to you, it's "no big deal"? How could you adjust your priorities to serve even more in this way?
4. Can you think of any reason that God doesn't create people who can "do it all"?
5. How does Philippians 1:6 help us continue the discipline necessary to find the sweet spot in our Divine Design?

CHAPTER 26

YOUR STATEMENT OF MISSION

The future is not some place we are going, but one we create. The paths are not found, but made, and the activity of making them changes both the maker and the destination.
— John Schaar

It's been listed as one of the deadliest train accidents ever. On March 2, 1944, train 8017 pulled out of its station in Italy. Not long after, almost all of its passengers – more than 500 people – were dead. The train didn't jump the tracks or explode or crash. In fact, the train suffered no external damage. So why did so many people die? As the train pulled into a long tunnel, it apparently began to lose traction. There in the dark tunnel, faced with the unknown, the engineers had to react to an unclear situation. Precisely what they did, no one knows for sure. But we do know they lacked the clarity to exit the tunnel quickly. Carbon monoxide fumes from the low-grade coal spewing out of the train's smokestack poisoned more than 500 people. Clarity empowers you to act decisively – and fast. So instead of being stuck in a dark, dangerous situation, debating what to do, you'll already know.

If each of us has been given something unique to do, then we must throw ourselves into it. But there are so many possibilities – far more opportunities than we have time, energy or resources for. One woman describes this well: ". . . working through my divine assignment . . . frees me to focus on just one thing. It seems I have been blessed (or perhaps cursed) with more good opportunities for work, fellowship, and family activities than I could possibly do and still come even close to enjoying them and be a decent person for my family to live with . . . If my assignment from God is to encourage I can give myself permission to say no to the things that don't fit within that scope."[1]

A first step in experiencing this kind of clarity is to write out your own mission statement. A personal mission statement is simply a one-sentence version of God's plan for your life. When you express this in an action-focused sentence, it will motivate you to pursue your plan. Here are some examples:

"I believe I am to write a series of children's books that will make a story at bedtime a lasting memory."

"I believe my divine assignment is to offer a listening ear to troubled youth and guide them into making life-affirming decisions."

"I believe I've been gifted to write music that will lift the soul and point it toward God."

"I believe my design is to encourage and inspire abused women to improve their self-esteem so that this devastating pattern is not passed on to their children."

"God has given me a dream to work with the politicians of our area in an effort to provide affordable housing to the poor and disadvantaged."

"I believe my divine assignment is to use my public speaking gifts to influence people to make personal decisions that are faith enhancing."

"For even the Son of Man did not come to be served, but to serve, and to give His life as a ransom for many" (Jesus, Mark 10:45).

As you can see from these examples, putting into words your statement of mission brings focus and clarity to daily activities. That's not to say your mission will never change. Recognize your statement as a working idea and that it is today's statement of your understanding of why God placed you on earth. In other words, where do you see God's fingerprints on your destiny? What is producing results in your life? What are people affirming? What is giving you peace and joy?

There are some days we care for our granddaughter while her mother, Angela, is at work. Alexa is a preschooler and when I come home from the office or an appointment I can generally tell when she's been there. She has a habit of pressing her face and hands against the windowpane to watch for "Pop-Pop's" arrival. Even if she's not at the door when I get home, I can see evidence that she's been there. Her mark is unmistakable – tongue prints, nose prints, fingerprints are all over the windowpanes surrounding our front door.

To help define your statement of mission you might ask yourself, "Where do people see my fingerprints? Where do I really make a difference? How do people know that I've been there?"

Even before we were born, God prepared good works for us to do (Ephesians 2:10). This work gets accomplished through the expression of our spiritual DNA. It's in our wiring. We will be restless until we line up our activities with the work God created us to do.

A kindergarten teacher was observing her classroom of children while they created a piece of artwork with crayons. The teacher stopped by the desk of a little girl whose diligent efforts were expressed with great intensity on her face. The teacher asked the little girl what she was drawing. "I'm drawing God," she said. The teacher paused and said, "But no one knows what God looks like." The little girl paused to look up from her drawing and expressed confidently, "They will when I'm done."

As a Christian your personal mission statement is actually a way of drawing God. People will understand more about Him as a result of the creative expressions of your life. After all, remember that your design is a divine one. It aligns with His purposes. When you pursue it with excellence, executing a mission that is uniquely yours, even when you're not present people will know that God has been there.

REFLECTION

1. Peter Drucker once said that everyone should be able to fit their life mission on a T-shirt. What would yours read?

2. How does your response to the question above fit into God's larger plan for the world?

3. Think back to how you would have written your personal statement of mission 10 years ago. How would it look different from today? What would you like it to look like 10 years from today?

4. In the classic movie *It's a Wonderful Life*, actor James Stewart gets the opportunity to see what the world would have looked like without him. What would the world look like without you? What would be missing?

5. Read John 8:31 and 32. Imagine how difficult life would be if Christ had not freed us from the power of sin. Which items on your personal mission statement would be missing were it not for Christ's work?

CHAPTER 27

IT'S ALL ABOUT SERVICE

As each one has received a special gift, employ it in serving one another.
–I Peter 4:10 (NASB)

Not since Copernicus has there been such a strong feeling that the world revolves around us. Up until 1543 fathers could place an arm around their children, point to the night sky and reveal this bit of wisdom: "The universe revolves around us." We later discovered the earth revolves around the sun and that we aren't the center of things, the sun is. Spiritually, the same is true. We aren't the center, the Son is. And God's Son, Jesus Christ, did not come to be served but to serve others. We are to do the same. In other words, our SHAPE is for service, not self-centeredness.

Discovering our Divine Design releases a surge of serving potential. When we come to Jesus Christ we enroll in the University of Service called Serve U.

God's plan for us to go high involves bowing low in service to others. It isn't always easy. Very often God places us within the constraints of a serving environment where we'd rather not go, to learn what we thought we already knew. We make our attempts at humility – but is anyone watching? Sometimes God tests our hearts by asking us to serve in a way that doesn't absolutely match our SHAPE. If you see someone trip with a bag of groceries, God isn't expecting you to say, "Sorry, I don't have the gift of mercy or helps." All of us are called to show compassion whether we have that gift or not.

Jesus took His mission, passion, gifts and personality and applied them to the service of others. To use your discoveries about your Divine Design effectively you must follow His example. He didn't use His gifts to make Himself a superstar but to push others forward. Joseph Shulam tells an amazing story of a man who simulated the actions of Jesus. Shulam is a pastor in Jerusalem who describes the son of a rabbi who battled severe emotional problems. One day the boy went into his backyard, removed all his clothing, crouched down and began to gobble like a turkey. This went on not just for hours or days, but for weeks. He would not listen to appeals and no psychotherapist was able to help him.

A friend of the rabbi, having watched the boy and sharing in his father's grief, offered to help. His approach was surprising. He went into the backyard and removed his clothes. He crouched beside the boy and began gobbling, turkey-like. For days, nothing changed. Finally, the friend spoke to the son. "Do you think it would be all right for turkeys to wear shirts?" After some thought and many gobbles, the son agreed. So they put on their shirts. Days later the friend asked the boy if it would be okay for turkeys to wear pants. The boy nodded. In time, the friend redressed the boy. And, in time, the boy returned to normal.[1]

Although this is an extreme example of bizarre behavior, must we have looked any different when the Creator of the heavens and earth took human form? Jesus surrendered the privileges of His heavenly state, entered our world, picked up a towel and began to serve. He got down on our level. If we are going to be effective, we must follow His model – humble service. F. B. Meyer states, "I used to think that God's gifts were on shelves – one above the other – and the taller we grow, the easier we can reach them. Now I find that God's gifts are on shelves – and the lower we stoop, the more we get."

It is through service that we pass on what we have been given. It is the way that we authentically share our lives with others. A number of years ago my son and I went to Papua, New Guinea, to build houses in the inner jungle as an outreach of Habitat for Humanity. The founder of this organization, Millard Fuller, provided me with an inspiring life credo. He said, "I see life as both a gift and a responsibility. My responsibility is to use what God has given me to help His people in need."

Francis of Assisi put it this way: "Keep a clear eye toward life's end. Do not forget your purpose and destiny as God's creature. What you are in His sight is what you are and nothing more. Remember that when you leave this earth, you can take nothing that you have received . . . but only what you have given: a full heart enriched by honest service, love, sacrifice and courage."[2] Don't focus on recognition for what you do. There are 750 halls of fame in America and 450 "who's who" publications, but the individuals they recognize aren't necessarily life's true servants. There is a difference between success and significance.

Your Divine Design begins with an inward evaluation that leads to an outward thrust. In other words, your Divine Design must be others-centered. It is God's way of helping you live beyond yourself.

Dietrich Bonhoeffer wrote:

> It is part of the discipline of humility that we must not spare our hand where it can perform a service and that we do not assume that our schedules are our own to manage, but allow it to be arranged by God.[3]

Our actions speak much louder than what we say. Paul put it this way:

> Each of you should look not only to your own interests, but also to the interests of others. Your attitude should be the same as that of Christ Jesus: who being in the very nature of God, did not consider equality with God something to be grasped, but made Himself nothing, taking the very nature of a servant, being made in human likeness. Philippians 2:4-7 (NIV)

As servants our only care is seeking the approval of the One we serve. By that I do not refer to just those in need, but to God Himself. Colossians 3:23 and 24 (NIV) says, "Whatever you do, work at it with all your heart, as working for the Lord, not for men, since you know you will receive an inheritance from the Lord as a reward. It is the Lord Christ you are serving."

No matter where we serve, we should do it with all our might. Martin Luther King, Jr., said, "If a man is called to be a street sweeper, he should sweep streets even as Michelangelo painted or as Beethoven composed music or Shakespeare wrote poetry. He should sweep streets so well that all the hosts of heaven and earth will pause to say, 'Here lived a great street sweeper who did his job well.' "[4]

Discovering your Divine Design is the next step in a life of effective service. It is a means of following the example of Christ. You can be sure you are exercising more of God's purpose for you if your capacity to serve is growing.

REFLECTION

1. If you were to design the curriculum for a course at Serve U, what would be the name of the course and its top three objectives?
2. Jesus bridged an unimaginable gap by taking his omnipotence and using it to serve humankind. Why do so many find it so hard to offer their strength to the disadvantaged?
3. If your life were to at this moment be evaluated on the basis of what you have left behind in service to others, would you be satisfied? What would you change?
4. Why do you think certain gifts and jobs are seen as "service" to others and some are not? Evaluate what you do on the basis of service.
5. Read Luke 22:27. How did this new measuring rod for success turn everything that had gone before it upside down? Several thousand years after this utterance, do we understand and practice it?

CHAPTER 28

READY TO RISK IT?

God doesn't want us to be shy with His gifts, but bold . . .
– II Timothy 1:7 (MES)

The decision to grow always involves a choice, and that choice is frequently between risk and comfort.

It's been said that the only mistake is to not risk making one. If you've been playing it safe with your life, it's time to step up and step out. It's time to open yourself up to new and better ways of living, taking into account your Divine Design. If you find others who are gifted in some of the same ways you are, they can advise you. Pursuing your passion may require trading what seems to be security with the risk of failure. Someone once stated, "One day will come when the risk it takes to remain tight in the bud will be more painful than the risk it takes to blossom." Why not today?

If you've read the Gospels even once you certainly know the risks of burying your talent. In Matthew 25 we find the story of a man who entrusts his wealth to his servants before taking a long journey. The Bible says he gave one five talents, another two and another one – according to their individual abilities. It's important to realize that before talent meant skill, it meant money. It was the largest unit of accounting in the Greek currency and was the equivalent of 10,000 denarii. (According to Matthew 20:2 one denarius represented a day's fair wages.) If you do the calculations to bring this sum into modern currency you would discover that one talent is essentially the equivalent of all your earnings over a lifetime. We can certainly infer from the story that your God-given design has a high heavenly market value. (I read recently that Wal-Mart estimates that the monetary impact of losing one customer's purchasing power over a lifetime is $215,000. As staggering as this seems, according to this story of the talents, you're worth far more than several hundred thousand dollars. You are actually a multi-million-dollar enterprise!)

The story tells us that the first two servants rewarded the trust of their master by trading their talents and doubling their investment. Both took risks and had their risks rewarded even though there were no guarantees of a return. And when their master returned they were commended and rewarded. According to the story, they were rewarded in like manner. They received equal praise though the amounts of their return were different based on the original amount invested. But we must remember the lesson uncovered in a study of the third servant. In verses 24 and 25 of Matthew 25 this servant confesses that he was afraid and went and hid his talent in the ground. Where the first two servants went and traded, the last one went and dug. I've heard the scene described in this way: "The first two went out on a limb. The third hugged the trunk." Invest for success or hurry and bury – which is the better choice? Based on the master's rebuke we may conclude it is a great danger and common mistake to fail to use our talents to the master's benefit.

Just as in the development of every other Christian virtue, we are faced with a choice – in this case fear or faith. Fear causes us to act selfishly and protect our own interests. Do we bury the gifts that we've been given out of fear that we will not get a return on our investment, or do we hold on to them, making them available for our own use?

Our family once was invited to a dinner in which the hostess served the most amazing soup. It was unlike anything I had ever tasted. And my avalanche of appreciation resulted in a take-home container filled with the leftovers. When I got into the house I carefully constructed a little open space in the back of a lower shelf of the refrigerator to hide my prized possession. We had five full-size appetites at the time and I feared that without concealing my treasure, I might never taste it again. The tinge of guilt I felt was quickly rationalized. After all, no one loved this dish as much as I did.

You may be able to guess the end of the story. Weeks later my wife commented on an unusual odor in the fridge. Silly me, I never made the connection. When she cleaned out the refrigerator, I was found out. With a squeal of displeasure she asked, "What on earth is this?" She took the lid off my soup to reveal an entirely new life form.

I was saddened and embarrassed that what had been offered as a free gift had been spoiled by my lack of generosity. No one enjoyed my beloved soup because I was so selfish. What I had received for free, I hoarded. And it hurt us all.

Sin at its core always seeks to steal heavenly gifts for selfish gain.

C. S. Lewis wrote:

Sin is the distortion of an energy breathed into us – an energy which, if not thus distorted would have blossomed into one of those holy acts whereof "God did it" and "I did it" are both true descriptions. We poison the wine as He decants it into us; murder the melody he would play with us as the instrument. We caricature the self-portrait He would paint. Hence all sin, whatever else it is, is sacrilege.[1]

Embedded in the story of the talents is the secret to overcoming fear of risk. When the master criticizes the one-talent servant for burying his resources, the servant offers this excuse: "I knew that you were a hard man, harvesting where you have not sown and gathering where you have not scattered. So I was afraid and went out and hid your gold in the ground." The master repeats the servant's assessment, with the exclusion of one portion. The servant had said, "I knew you were a hard man," but the master wouldn't repeat an analysis he wouldn't accept. Would a hard master give multimillion-dollar gifts to undeserving servants and then honor them for their bold initiatives? Of course not.

The point is that the one-talent servant never really knew the intent of the master. Even though he had related to him regularly, he had a dim view of the master's heart, and as a result, he broke it. Servants who take risks with their God-given gifts and talents are those who know the master to be a merciful, loving and gracious provider.

Our daughter took us to the famed St. Andrew's Cathedral in Amalfi, Italy. The cathedral was certainly beautiful, but the biggest surprise was in the basement. As we wandered down a dark and damp corridor we began to notice some of the most amazing busts, artwork and sculptures we had ever seen. I couldn't help but wonder why all these masterpieces were down in the basement. Why not bring them out to where they could be seen and appreciated?

Perhaps God is asking you the very same question. You might be unwittingly keeping His masterpiece hidden away from the eyes of the world. It's certainly not what He wants. God intends for you to take the risks necessary to bring your talents and abilities onto the world's stage. Don't bury your talent. While there is a risk in investing it for the Master's sake, it brings great reward.

REFLECTION

1. Albert Einstein said, "Your imagination is the preview to life's coming attractions." Describe the role you think the imagination plays in faith and risk.

2. Describe an occasion when you took a significant risk – what was the outcome? As the years go by, do you find yourself taking fewer risks or more? Explain.

3. Sometimes limiting our time frame brings focus to our activities. If you had one year to live, how would you make the most of it?

4. What are some of the areas God is identifying in your life that are risk-worthy? What would need to happen for you to step out in these areas?

5. Read about Moses' experience in Hebrews 11:24-27. What risk was he willing to take to pursue his vision? Where do you think his strength came from?

CHAPTER 29

FAITH TO IMPLEMENT

Everyone has his own specific vocation or mission in life. Everyone must carry out a concrete assignment that demands fulfillment. Therein he cannot be replaced, nor can his life be repeated. Thus everyone's task is as unique as his specific opportunity to implement it.
    —Viktor Frankl

Developing a new perspective on your life will be challenging. There will be a sense in which you feel out of control.

I will never forget my first skiing experience. I went with a group of teens and an adult leader who was a great skier but a poor trainer. His guidance pretty much consisted of "Take the lift up and then I'll meet you at the bottom." I got in the line for what I was soon to learn was a "T-bar." It was not a seat but just a narrow piece of wood that tucked under your bottom and pulled you to the top. Halfway up the mountain it dawned on me that all the T-bars on the other side of the lift were coming back empty. I soon realized you had to ski off the lift. My exit was more of a jump and a squat so that the T-bar didn't hit me in the back of the head. Unfortunately I was still facing the upside of the mountain – momentarily. It was fading from view as I increased speed going down the mountain . . . backward!

I don't know how I did it but somehow on my way down I got myself turned around just in time to see that I was about to hit someone who had chosen that moment to sidestep across the trail. With my razor-sharp reflexes I drew upon another sport, squatted into a ball and took out the person as though he were a bowling pin. But I had never heard language that foul at the alleys. The part I understood sounded like "Why didn't you let me know you were coming?" And if I hadn't swallowed my tongue I would have yelled back, "Because I was scared!" When we engage in new behaviors, we often feel out of control and fear we may hurt ourselves and others. But there is no faster way to make progress.

Let's get more specific. When we risk doing things in new ways, when we "step out in faith," it is not in a vacuum. It is true there are certain conditions necessary for giftedness to thrive. Place a polar bear on a tropical beach or a parakeet on a polar ice cap and the clock begins ticking toward their end. But God has already placed us in a constellation of friends and surrounded us with opportunities that are a part of His plan for us. So even when we feel all alone and threatened, He is there to guide us. We must take the plunge. In her book *The Eighth Day of Creation*, Elizabeth O'Connor writes, "We cannot fool ourselves for long about what we are to do. Somewhere deep down in us is stored the secret, and when we are digging in the wrong place, we know it. The secret wants to be discovered and will not let us go in peace a way that is not ours."[1]

Your design affects your perception of what is around you. It is likely that you actually interpret the realities around you in a way that suits your particular makeup and design. For example, let's imagine a gathering such as a wedding reception. The master of ceremonies, who enjoys the attention of a crowd, sees an audience. A politician attending may see votes. A soloist may see a roomful of critics. An event planner sees a half-dozen things that may contribute to a delay. And, of course, the bride and groom see not only a loving and adoring crowd, but a table of waiting-to-be-opened presents.

When we use our faith to step more fully into our Divine Design, we are actually motivated to do so on the basis of our internal wiring. Following these inclinations is most likely to produce success. Tell me what you've been designed to do and I can predict that a large amount of faith will be expressed in that arena.

And remember, faith is developed through times of testing. An inquiring man once met a wise counselor on his journey toward success. The man asks the counselor, "Which way is success?"

The bearded man doesn't speak but points to a place in the distance. The man, thrilled by the prospect of quick and easy success, rushes off. Suddenly, there comes a loud "splat." Eventually, the man, now tattered and stunned, limps back, assuming he must have taken a wrong turn. He repeats his question to the counselor, who again points silently in the same direction.

The man obediently walks off, and this time the splat sound is deafening. When the man crawls back, he is bloody, broken and irate. "I asked you which way to success!" he screams at the counselor. "I followed your directions, and all I got was splatted! No more of this pointing! Talk!"

The counselor does speak, and what he says is this: "Success is that way. Just a little past splat."

Are you willing to have your faith developed sufficiently that it will take you past splat? Martin Luther King, Jr., said, "The measure of a man is not where he stands in moments of convenience, but where he stands in times of challenge and adversity."

Hebrews 11:30 says, "By faith the walls of Jericho fell after the people marched around them for seven days." The story of Joshua and Jericho is one of my favorites. Right after crossing into the Promised Land, the Israelites faced a walled city. Without weapons and untrained in warfare, they faced one of the world's strongest fortifications. God tells them to walk around the city once a day for six days and say nothing, but on the seventh day, to march around it seven times, thanking God for His answer. Imagine what your average Israelite slave felt on those first six days as the vicious warriors of Jericho sneered down on them. But by faith, they persevered and in the right time, they had their answer. You may feel walled in or out. It may seem like you've been waiting for your answer forever. It's hard to be discouraged when you know God is in control. When we are unsure of our direction, God expects us to trust Him by faith. The more faith you use, the more it grows. The more it grows, the greater your exploits in pursuit of your Divine Design.

Reflection

1. Describe your first attempt at something new. What emotions did you feel? How did you cope? What was the outcome?
2. Why is using our Divine Design in a new area of service often very difficult? Is this evidence that you don't understand your design or that you just need more time to practice?
3. Give an example of something that you currently do well but earlier in your life had failed at.
4. Is it possible that there are opportunities for service that you currently turn down because of a bad experience years back? Should your growing faith cause you to step out in some of these areas once again?
5. David says in I Samuel 17:47, "The battle is the Lord's." How do you determine what is your responsibility and what is God's responsibility when you implement your Divine Design?

CHAPTER 30

FINDING THE SPARK

The person who wakes up and finds himself a success hasn't been asleep.
—Wilson Mizner, U.S. dramatist

A spark is created by rubbing two objects together. One of the objects has the potential to ignite and be transformed – that's us. The other object is relatively unalterable – the world around us.

In the Middle Ages before the days of matches, lighting a fire from scratch was a difficult process. As a result, people often carried with them a metal box containing a smoldering cinder, which they kept alight throughout the day with little bits of kindling. This would mean that people could light a fire wherever they went because they carried their own personal spark.

God intends our universe to be alive with sparks that are ready to light the possibilities of our passion. T. E. Lawrence stated, "All men dream . . . but not equally. They who dream by night in the dusty recesses of their minds wake in the day to find that it is all vanity; but the dreamers of the day are dangerous men, for they act their dream with open eyes to make it possible."

But many sparks can be extinguished by a wrong attitude. A negative attitude can make a difficult circumstance even worse. That's what happened to Bob. Bob's car ran out of gasoline while traveling through the Iowa countryside. He thought he remembered seeing a farmhouse two miles back, so he started walking. Then it started to rain. Feeling sorry for himself, he began imagining negative scenarios. Nobody would be home. Or the farmer would be home, but asleep, and Bob would have to wake him up. From there he imagined the farmer available but simply not willing to help him. Bob was working up a sweat. He went on a "comparison trip." He imagined the farmer in a nice warm bed resting comfortably while he was soaking wet and tired, with a car that wouldn't run. His heart was racing from the stress and anger, not from the walk.

By the time Bob saw the farmhouse he was furious. He pounded on the door with his fist. From an upstairs window the innocent farmer asked, "Who's there?"

An irrational Bob snapped back, "You know who it is, and I wouldn't take any gasoline from you if you had the last gallon on earth!" With that he stomped off, completely soaked and steaming mad. Bob's imagination had closed the door to opportunity. Many opportunities are missed because we focus on the result rather than the process.[1] This may cause us to give up too soon.

Long before Alexander Graham Bell invented the telephone, a German schoolteacher named Reese almost did. Reese's phone could convey sounds of whistling and humming, but not speech. Something was missing. Many years later when Reese had given up, Bell discovered his error. A tiny screw that controlled the electrodes was off by a thousandth of an inch. When Bell made this minor adjustment he was able to transmit speech loud and clear.

Think about it – an adjustment so small that you could barely measure it spelled the difference between success and failure – and changed history![2] Abraham Lincoln wrote, "Success is going from failure to failure without losing your enthusiasm."

To find the spark in your life, you must be persistent. Remember the example of Moses. Hebrew 11:29 (NIV) says, "By faith he . . . persevered because he saw Him who is invisible." Moses realized the importance of seeing in his mind's eye what was invisible to his natural eye. By faith he visualized his goal. He refused to give up until he saw in front of him what God had promised. Moses had tremendous endurance.

Imagine that your dreams are library books. Some of the books in the library are fiction, as are some of your dreams. Some of the books are for reference, some of them are about your aspirations, your hopes for the future, and some of the books are textbooks that teach you lessons. Some of the books are thick, some are thin, some are hardbound and some are paperback. The true point of your reading, of course, is to gain sufficient understanding so that you can actually accomplish something. But you may have a problem. Right now you're not sure what you're looking for. You're uncertain about what's going to create a spark to help you accomplish your dream. Your ideas are in disarray like library books that have been dumped into the after-hours book bin. In order to rightly return these books to their appropriate and organized shelves, they need to be sorted. With greater organization, focus, and vision in your life you will be able to persevere, until you achieve your desired goal.

Jot down the location of the sparks in your life and work to clarify them. Don't hesitate to present your desires to God. After all, He knows what it feels like to be us. David says to God in Psalm 38:9: "All my longings lie open before You, Oh Lord; my sighing is not hidden from you."

As you continue to develop the right attitude to persevere and to present those inklings of your dreams and passions to God, you will soon find that your spark is beginning to burn more brightly.

God never gives you a job to do without giving you a divine spark. That passion may be lying dormant in you until you discover and develop it. A spark carries with it the power to bless others. When we fan it into flame (the subject of the next chapter) it can have unexpected and perhaps eternal impact.

REFLECTION

1. Who has helped you recognize the spark within? Who have you helped?
2. Have you ever had a dream extinguished? Was it due to your attitude or outside forces?
3. How would you advise someone who asked you for a three-point plan to launch a dream?
4. Do you spend much time using your imagination? Does it result in anything productive or just fantasies?
5. Read Proverbs 9:10. How does this verse relate to staying "fired up" as you pursue your Divine Design?

CHAPTER 31

FANNING THE FLAME

You are free to choose, but the choices you make today will determine what you will have, be and do in the tomorrow of your life.
– Zig Ziglar

Sparks are of little benefit themselves. They've got to be fanned into flame. Paul says in II Timothy 1:6 to "Fan into flame the gift of God." The assumption in this verse is that the gift has been identified. In I Corinthians 12:7 Paul states that the gifts are not just for us, but are to be used to help others. In the following chapter he describes our highest pursuit as believers – love for one another. And then in I Corinthians 14:1 Paul brings the two ideas together: "Follow the way of love and eagerly desire spiritual gifts." Obviously the early Christians were to know what their spiritual gifts were and they were to desire them because they are important.

The best way I know to do this is through worship. When you use the gifts that God has given you, it is actually an act of worship. When you are doing what you have been wired and shaped to do and you do it in a way that benefits other people, you are reflecting God's creativity and it brings Him glory. In fact, John 15:8 states that when you produce much fruit, God is honored and glorified. In other words, the use of your gifts fans the flame to expand the use of your gifts. When you don't use them, you lose them. According to psychologist Abraham Maslow, "The story of the human race is the story of men and women selling themselves short."

The Bible says in Romans 6:13 that we are to give ourselves completely to God since we have been given new life and we are to use our whole body as a tool to do what is right for the glory of God. Leon Fleischer, renowned pianist and teacher, has said that playing a piece of music is an exercise in antigravity. The musician's role is to draw the listener's attention over the bar lines – which are but artificial divisions, having no relevance to the flow of the music – toward a realization of the piece as a whole.[1] There's a sense in which our service is an exercise in antigravity. The goal is not to focus on the individual act or even the person performing it but to see that the flow of service is an expression, an offering, if you will, to our Creator.

Unfortunately, many people use their gifts for their own purposes rather than God's. Either they use them to get attention and acclaim from others or they use them selfishly and for their own ends. They use their gifts for and on themselves. So the talented accountant shows no interest in assisting others in developing wise and balanced budgets but is interested only in his billable hours. The gifted arbitrator cares little about justice but wants only to win the maximum number of cases so that he can become partner and be elevated to the next pay grade.

To sustain passion, to have your gifts, abilities and energies be fanned into a raging fire, you must take what you've been given and present it back to God. Martha Graham is quoted as having said:

> There is a vitality, a life force, an energy, a quickening that is translated through you into action, and because there is only one of you and all of time, this expression is unique. And if you block it, it will never exist through any other medium and it will be lost. The world will not have it. It is not your business to determine how good it is nor how valuable nor how it compares with other expressions. It is your business to keep . . . the channel open.[2]

It's sad that many people spend much of their lives envying the gifts and talents of other people without ever putting their own into practice. You might say that failing to use our gifts or envying the gifts of others actually detracts from the worship of God. The word *joy* and the word *gift* actually come from the same original word. It's the word for *grace*. No feeling compares to being used by God, and that's why the more people use their gifts, the more they want to use them. It helps to fan the flame.

"Is it possible to be used too much?" you may ask. It is important to mention that burning up is not the same as burning out. We can be consumed by our passion, and that's why it's called a passion. Following this path will touch others.

We've lived in our neighborhood 25 years. For 24 of them we burned logs in a wood stove for supplemental heat during Pennsylvania's cold winters. At a recent neighborhood picnic, one of our neighbors said, "We miss it."

"Miss it?" I asked.

"The smell of your stove in the chilly night air. We could always tell when you were burning."

Through several decades of conversations (our kids were best friends) we never realized that our neighbors were receiving small, smoke-filled delights through the efforts of our "burn." You may not think that being consumed by the passion of your Divine Design is having much of an impact on anyone but you, but it is. Nearly imperceptible smoke and ash is flowing out your life's chimney and having a spiritual impact on your relational neighborhood.

REFLECTION

1. Why do you think so many people take the gifts God has given them and hide them or use them only on themselves?
2. How does envying the gifts of others dampen your own flame? Give an example of this occurring in your own life.
3. How persistent are you in the pursuit of a dream? What lessons have you learned that help to keep you from giving up?
4. If there were a graveyard for dead dreams, would you have made use of it? What would some of the tombstones read?
5. Read Isaiah 43:1-3. How do these verses motivate you to persist in the pursuit of your Divine Design?

CHAPTER 32

A RAGING FIRE

*If I were to wish for anything I should not wish for wealth and power, but for
the passionate sense of what can be, for the eye, which, ever young and ardent,
sees the possible. Pleasure disappoints, possibility never. And what wine is so
sparkling, what so fragrant, what so intoxicating as possibility?*
— Søren Kierkegaard, *Either/Or*

In the beginning, it is written, was the Word. Problem was, nobody
was listening. There's a story waiting to be told, but most aren't aware of its
importance. It's a story of passion and redemption, of soul searching and
surrender, of gifts given and talent invested. The scope of this drama plays
out through the ages and you have a part.

In fact, you play a key role and some lines will ring hollow unless ut-
tered by your voice. Will you accept the script? The guest of honor hopes
so – because He is coming to see you in a one-of-a-kind performance of the
ages.

How will you find the energy and motivation required? How do you
tap into the power source – where do you find the electric socket for sus-
tained current?

It may surprise you to know that the Bible talks about a "power that
is at work in you" (Ephesians 3:20). The question you have to ask yourself
is this: Is that power working in you, or is it just residing in you? You may
have all the potential in the world, but God doesn't act on your behalf based
on your potential. He acts according to your faith as demonstrated by your
actions. In my book *Emerging Faith* I state that there is a direct relationship
between our level of trust in God and what we see Him do in our lives. If
we place more confidence in Him we will see greater evidence of His help,
which in turn will encourage us to have even more faith.

When you are trusting God to fulfill a dream or passion He's given
you, there is a progression He usually follows. First, He gives you a promise.
Next, He gives you a plan. Third, He allows you to face a problem, and
then, finally, we see a demonstration of His power.

Think back to the Old Testament example of Abraham. God told him
that He would multiply his offspring like grains of sand on a seashore. That
was the promise. Then God gave him a plan, which included having him

leave his country, changing his name and giving him a son. The chapters of the book of Genesis are dedicated to describing the problems Abraham faced in realizing his plan. But the outcome was sure. God's power was demonstrated and His promise fulfilled.

God promised Moses that He would be with him wherever he went as long as he followed God's plan to free the Israelites. There was the problem of the plagues, the problem of the desert, the problem of the murmuring people before Moses arrived at his "promised" land.

Jesus gave the disciples a promise that He would be with them to the end of the age. The plan that He gave them was to go and make disciples of all nations. The problem was, not everybody was receptive to becoming a Christ-follower. Nonetheless, as the disciples continued to trust God, His power was demonstrated and, through the ages, billions of people have become Christians.

Many people receive God's promise and plan but are unwilling to go through a problem that strengthens their faith and ultimately leads to the release of power. One Christian prayed for years, "Give me more power, more power!" Finally God said, "With plans no bigger than yours, you don't need more power."

Are you pursuing your Divine Design with such dedication and passion that the things God's calling you to do cannot be accomplished unless He shows up? Are you planning to do things so great that they cannot be attributed simply to your own human ability?

If you hope to see God's purpose for your life stoked into a raging fire, then don't limit your faith in God's ability to provide. Believe for the plan and promise of your dream and be willing to face any obstacles that get in the way through faith and trust.

Most great achievers have discovered that there is a wellspring of help and hope beyond themselves. Looking only within yourself can leave you frustrated and wanting. Even the 12 apostles couldn't have pulled off their assignments on the basis of their own strength and ability.

To: Son of Joseph
WoodCrafters Carpenter Shop
Nazareth 25922

From: Jordan Management Consultants
Jerusalem 26544

Subject: Staff Team Evaluation

Thank you for submitting the resumes of the 12 men you have picked for management positions in your new organization. All of them have now taken our battery of tests; and we have not only run the results through our computer, but also arranged personal interviews for each of them with our psychologist and vocational aptitude consultant.

It is the staff opinion that most of your nominees are lacking in background, education and vocational aptitude for the type of enterprise you are undertaking. They do not have the team concept. We would recommend that you continue your search for persons of experience in managerial ability and proven capacity.

Simon Peter is emotionally unstable and given to fits of temper.

Andrew has absolutely no qualities of leadership.

The two brothers, James and John, the sons of Zebedee, place personal interest above company loyalty.

Thomas demonstrates a questioning attitude that would tend to undermine morale.

We feel it is our duty to tell you that Matthew has been black-listed by the Greater Jerusalem Better Business Bureau.

James, the son of Alphaeus, and Thaddaeus have radical leanings, and they both registered a high score on the manic-depressive scale.

One of the candidates, however, shows great potential. He is a man of ability and resourcefulness, meets people well, has a keen business mind and has contacts in high places. He is highly motivated, ambitious and responsible. We recommend Judas Iscariot as your controller and right-hand man. All of the other profiles are self-explanatory. We wish you every success in your new venture . . .[1]

As Paul stated in I Corinthians 1:26: "Not many of you were wise by human standards; not many were influential; not many were of noble birth."

If we're counting on our own abilities and strengths to do a God-sized job, we're going to be bitterly disappointed. A consuming fire of passion requires an all-consuming God. He has everything you need to get you to His promised destination. For millennia He's been showing Himself strong for those who place their trust in Him. Will you?

REFLECTION

1. Can you give an example from your own life of a passionate start but a murmur of a finish? What could you have done differently to sustain your motivation?

2. Talking about your dream is great, but the faith to accomplish it comes from moving into action. What dreams have you failed to put into action?

3. What is the risk in failing to develop your Divine Design? How much time per week do you think it deserves?

4. Do you have inspiring examples that encourage you when you get weary and want to give up? Who, in your circle of relationships, sets the pace for persistence and passion? What could you learn from them?

5. Read II Timothy 1:6. Fire is known for its tendency to spread rapidly. Explain how a proper response to your Divine Design can impact others.

CHAPTER 33

SUSTAINING THE GAINS

Learn to define yourself, to content yourself with some specific thing and some definite work; dare to be what you really are, and to learn to accept with good grace all that you are not.
— Anonymous

Discovering your Divine Design and dedicating that discovery back to God is not the end of the story. The next step is critical, and that is to work at refining and developing that design. Our gifts and abilities are like muscles; the more we use them, the stronger they become and the more they can accomplish.

It's been said that no horse goes anywhere until he's harnessed; no steam drives anything until it's confined; no river generates any electricity until it's channeled. Likewise, no life ever grows great until it is focused, dedicated, and disciplined. Many men and women fail to leave a legacy of influence because they do not concentrate their energies and talents into specific areas.

Any gift and ability that God has given you is meant to be developed. If you would have told me when I was a teenager that I had the gift of public speaking and would be able to hold the attention of thousands of people, I would have laughed. I had some public speaking courses in high school and college and I was certainly not exceptional. And I didn't have any drive to speak in front of crowds. But embedded deep within me, I soon discovered, was a core capacity critical to those who would speak in front of an audience. I was not afraid to step in front of a crowd and command their attention.

But being unafraid to speak in front of others and having something worthy to say are two distinctly different things. After being trained in theology I had greater confidence that I had something to say. But I was applying my learning mostly one-on-one until someone tapped me on the shoulder and said, "I was wondering if you would speak to our group." My willingness, combined with a God-given capacity to be fearless in front of crowds, combined with dedication to learn something worth saying, produced this public speaker.

But it took years and years of dedicating that gift back to God and practicing with it before I would say I was effective. For over 20 years we've been doing multiple services at our church, which means that a prepared message gets not only multiple rehearsals but multiple presentations. At one point in our history when we were meeting in a much smaller facility, I would do six services between Saturday night and Sunday. That's a lot of practice. So when someone refers to what they call my "natural gift" of speaking in front of others, I think of the thousands of hours that I've dedicated to my craft. In my case, becoming an "overnight success" took about 30 years. I still don't think of myself as having an exceptional public speaking gift. I simply had a willingness to develop a skill in an area where God had gifted me.

When someone compliments me on a presentation, I think back to my first one when with a dramatic swoop of my hand I knocked over the music stand holding my notes and never quite recovered. I was encouraged when a few people asked me when I was speaking again. It wasn't until later that I found out it was so they could avoid being there. Or the time when I had to stop talking and ask the audience to pray for me because I was so hopelessly lost in the muddle of my own words. Developing your gifts may not be a smooth process. At least it wasn't for me.

Philadelphia is a city known as much for its rabid fans as its sports teams. After watching the ebb and flow of these teams over the last couple of decades I've come to the conclusion that even the best team loses a lot of games and even the worst team has moments of brilliance. After a loss, very often the coaches will come out saying, "The most important thing is to have the team ready to play its next game." The most important thing to remember to sustain the gains you are making is to be ready for the next serving opportunity. So many fail to prepare. They stare up the steps rather than step up the stairs.

One of my favorite stories is about a farmer whose mule fell into a well. Since there was no way to get him out, the farmer decided to bury him there. But the mule had a different idea. Initially, when the shovelfuls of dirt started landing on his back, he became hysterical. Then this thought struck him: "Just shake it off, and step on it." So he did. Hour after hour, as the dirt fell on him, he kept telling himself, "Just shake it off and step on it." No matter how much dirt they threw on him, he just kept shaking it off and stepping on it until finally he stepped triumphantly out of the well. Life will either bury you or bless you, and very often the difference is having the right perspective. Paul put it this way in Romans 8:37: "In all these things, we are more than conquerors . . ." Don't give up.

No gift comes fully developed. It comes into your life in a certain way, but the more you use it, the more it develops. By practice, by learning, by studying you get better and better at it. There seems to be a law of abundance written into the framework of the universe that dictates that if you are given something and use it well, you get more of it. Try to get things too quickly and without work and you are likely to be disappointed. Jesus said that if we're faithful with little we'll be given much![1] It's the way that we sustain our gains.

REFLECTION

1. Sometimes people feel there is too much of an emphasis in our society on success. What does success mean to you? Do you think God wants us to excel?

2. Describe the process that was used to involve you in an area that now seems to be your specialty. Was the process planned or random? As you look back, do you think God was involved?

3. A national Gallup poll survey on volunteerism in America reported that the average volunteer serves about four to five hours a week. (This includes believers and nonbelievers alike.) Do you think believers should be serving more than nonbelievers? What is the average number of hours per week that you volunteer your time? Do you think this number should be lower or higher?

4. Give a personal example of how the repeated use of a skill, gift or talent resulted in greater opportunities for service.

5. Read Psalm 126:3. How does reviewing God's faithfulness in the past help us to face our future? Can you give a personal example?

CHAPTER 34

DOUBTS, DEFEATS
AND DISCOURAGEMENTS

*We are pressed on every side by troubles, but not crushed and broken. We are
perplexed because we don't know why things happen as they do, but we don't
give up and quit. We are hunted down, but God never abandons us. We get
knocked down, but we get up again and keep going.*
— II Corinthians 4:8, 9 (TLB)

You can be the most sincere and dedicated person the world has ever
seen, but that does not remove you from facing doubts, defeats and discouragements. Thomas Carlyle said, "The block of granite that was an obstacle
in the pathway of the wheat becomes a stepping stone in the pathway of the
straw."

Your life will be filled with mountains, with hurdles, with obstacles but
you get to decide how you respond to them. Failure is never final, nor is it
fatal. In Proverbs 24:16 the Bible says, "For a righteous man may fall seven
times and rise again." There's nothing wrong with being down, but there
is something wrong with staying down. You may be temporarily detoured,
but only you can make you stop. Austin O'Malley asserted, "The fact that
you've been knocked down is interesting, but the length of time you remain
down is important."

Coaches Landry, Noll, and Walsh accounted for nine of the 15 Super Bowl victories between 1974 and 1989. Do you know what else they
have in common? They also had the worst first-season records of any head
coaches in NFL history. If judged only on their first attempts, they probably all should have quit. Life isn't a snapshot; it's a moving picture.

No matter how long your struggle may last, it is not everlasting. One
week it may seem like you are making dramatic progress and the next week
you may experience drastic setbacks. There will be times when you get
tired, frustrated and depressed. You may even want to quit.

You shouldn't be surprised at the fiery darts hurled at you, for just as
much as God wants you to fulfill your destiny for your life, you have a spiritual enemy that wants the exact opposite. John 10:10 states that while Jesus
came to give us an abundant life, Satan comes to steal, kill and destroy. The
enemy of our soul takes great delight in purposeless, directionless,

selfish, wasted lives. He will try every trick in the book to keep you from discovering and developing your Divine Design. He may use materialism, the possibility of fame, greed, pleasure or pride, and if none of those work, complacency will do. There will be times when you may wonder whether God has actually gifted you at all and, if so, to what purpose. You may just want to give up.

Have you seen the movie about the talking animals titled *Babe*? It's Christmas Day on the farm. The pig, cow, hens, and Ferdinand, the duck, crowd by the kitchen window, craning their necks to see which unfortunate one of their kind has been chosen to become the main course of dinner. On the platter is Roseanna, a duck, dressed with sauce l'orange.

> Duck (Ferdinand): Why Roseanna? She had such a beautiful nature. I can't take it anymore! It's too much for a duck. It eats away at the soul . . .

> Cow: The only way to find happiness is to accept that the way things are is the way things are.

> Duck: The way things are stinks!

While the cow expresses an often-cited platitude, truth be told, the duck speaks for most of us. The circumstances seem so bad we just want to quit.

Many times we blame ourselves. "If I was only better at this or stronger at that . . ." But our weaknesses and imperfections were never meant to stop us in our tracks but provide the soil in which additional growth and insight can occur. God has used many in the Bible who might have used their life situation as an excuse for not fulfilling their Divine Design. Abraham was old, Jacob was insecure, Joseph was abused, Moses stuttered, Gideon was poor, Rahab was immoral, David had an affair, Elijah was depressed, Naomi was a widow, the Samaritan woman had several failed marriages, Zacchaeus was unpopular, Thomas had doubts, and on and on the list goes. In II Corinthians 12:9 (NIV) the apostle Paul reminds us that God can work through, not just in spite of, our weaknesses: "[But God] said to me, 'My grace is sufficient for you, for My power is made perfect in weakness.'"

Helen Keller said, "The marvelous riches of human experience would lose something of rewarding joy if there were no limitations to overcome. The hilltop tour would not be so wonderful if there were not dark valleys to traverse." A visit to Rome can reveal some striking contrasts. You can be dazzled by St. Peter's Basilica, the famed Sistine Chapel and the incomparable works of Michelangelo. But did you know that down the street, across from the Roman forum, you can find the notorious Mamertine Prison? This dungeon is believed to be where Paul resided while writing his letters to Timothy. Imagine him, feet bound, open to rain and cold through an iron gate, air barely breathable. Imagine him writing as he does in I Timothy 6:12 to fight the good fight of faith and not give up. All of us have had some Sistine Chapel experiences, but very often we feel as though life has us imprisoned. The crisis that you experience today may be a catalyst for God's purpose for you tomorrow.

In his book *Shaped by God*, author Max Lucado states, "God sees our life from beginning to end. He may lead us through a storm at age 30 so we can endure a hurricane at age 60."[1]

Perhaps what we need most at these times is perspective. While we focus on our faults and failures there's a much bigger story to consider. I think of the organizers of the National Spelling Bee who, every year at the finals, have to provide a "comfort room" where children who have spelled hundreds of words perfectly can go to cry, throw things and be comforted by their parents when they finally make one mistake. The hundreds of correct words are forgotten as they fail for having gotten one word wrong.[2] A focus on doing everything right (even for God) is bound to end in frustration. Harold Kushner cautions that life is not meant to be a spelling bee, "where one mistake wipes out all the things we've done right. Life is not a test for which the passing grade is 100 percent and anything less is a failure."[3] We are God's students, not life's victims.

A story is told about a famous pub in Europe. It was a beautiful, quaint little pub until one day a glass of wine was spilled onto one of the walls. The stain was unsightly, and the owner was distressed over the mess. One of the patrons of the pub happened to be a local artist. With supplies in hand and a vision in his heart for what could happen with the ugly stain on the wall, he began to transform gross imperfection into something beautiful. All night he worked. The next day when the pub opened for customers, they were treated to and delighted by a breathtaking masterpiece, the center of which, now barely distinguishable as such, was the formerly wretched stain. The moral? Impossible, messy, wretched mistakes can be transformed through the vision and touch of a master artist.

Euripides said, "Adversity calls forth the soul's courage to bear unflinchingly whatever Heaven sends." A great spirit will meet calamity in a great way.

It may be best when discovering, dedicating and developing your Divine Design that you regard adversity as your ally.

REFLECTION

1. Describe how your attitude toward failure, defeat and setbacks has changed as you have grown in your Christian life.

2. This book has addressed the relationship between your strengths and your Divine Design. Where do weaknesses come into play?

3. If opposition produces faith and faith helps to develop character (see James 1:2-4), is it possible that through difficulties God is not redirecting you, but providing you with the needed strength for the next step in your Divine Design? How do you know when to quit and when to persist?

4. If God were to take a life stain of yours (see the story above) and make it into something beautiful, which stain would He pick and what would He make it into?

5. Read James 1:3. Give an example of how this has occurred in your life.

CHAPTER 35

LIFE'S PRIORITIES AND CHOICES

. . . God made us plain and simple, but we have made ourselves very complicated.
— Ecclesiastes 7:29 (TEV)

If you've gotten this far in *Discovering Your Divine Design*, your head may be swimming with all kinds of thoughts. One of them may be *Where am I going to find the time to focus on my God-given SHAPE when I have so many other things on my plate?* It was Peter Drucker who said, "First things first and last things not at all." You are certainly not alone in your struggle with overload.

In 1880, Samuel Plimsoll of the United Kingdom tackled the problem of overloaded ships that were sinking in heavy seas. He submitted a bill in parliament insisting that a line be drawn on the outside of the hull of all British ships. When the ships were loaded with freight and reached the level where the line hit the water, they were not to be loaded with any more cargo. The marking on the ships' hull became known as the Plimsoll line.

We all have Plimsoll lines, although they are invisible. Very often they are drawn right under our nose and on some days we pray that no one makes a ripple.

It will be impossible for you to fulfill God's plan without knowing your limits and establishing certain priorities. Here are some questions that may help:

- Where could my gifts and abilities be most leveraged for Kingdom purposes to make the greatest difference?
- If I were to develop these gifts, what should get attention first?
- Are there areas of character development that are going to hinder my progress? If so, what shall I do about it?
- Do I need a specific skill?
- Where do I turn for help?
- What part of my plan am I most excited about?

Stephen Covey says, "It's easy to say 'No!' when there's a deeper 'Yes!' burning inside." He goes on to say that anything less than a conscious commitment to the important is an unconscious commitment to the unimportant.[1]

The problem is that there are just too many good causes and worthwhile endeavors for you to pursue in one lifetime. If you try to do them all, you will eventually become less and less effective. You must never let the things that matter most be at the mercy of those that matter least.

We are all diners at life's buffet. The problem is, we cannot put everything on our plate. We must be selective if we hope to enjoy our meal. The possibilities in your life and experiences that you will be offered are limitless, so we must be careful about our choices. Christians often have the most difficult time staying focused because they are susceptible to requests for help. Very often they submit themselves to fulfilling what God has called others to do, not what God has called them to do. Sadly, most people work very hard at things that do not fit their skills, ability and interests.

Bob Bufford says the only way to counter this is to "say no to anything that doesn't maximize these areas [of your design] even though it is only five or ten degrees off your mission."[2] In Al Ries's book *Focus*, the introduction begins with these lines: "The sun is a powerful source of energy. Every hour the sun washes the earth with billions of kilowatts of energy. Yet with a hat and some sunscreen, you can bathe in the light of the sun for hours at a time with few ill effects. A laser is a weak source of energy. A laser takes a few watts of energy and focuses them in a coherent stream of light. But with a laser, you can drill a hole in a diamond or wipe out a cancer."[3] Focus has power. Focusing on your priorities will bring laser-like results. But we must scan the horizon carefully before we select our areas of focus.

The fact that we should be selective in choosing where to focus doesn't mean that we shouldn't be open to unexpected ways that we can make a contribution. Life presents us with unexpected opportunities, and we must have enough discretionary time to take advantage of them. One example of this is found in the biblical story of the Good Samaritan, as told by Jesus in Luke 10. When a Jewish man walking from Jerusalem to Jericho gets mugged and is left bleeding at the side of the road, two religious leaders walk by and ignore his need. While his own kind ignored him, a Samaritan (who would be expected to have great animosity toward the Jews) not only tends to him, but puts him on his donkey, takes him to an inn and pays for his stay during his recovery.

I'm sure the Samaritan didn't say, "I don't have the gift of compassion." He had enough of a margin in his time and finances to help, even though he had a clear sense of priority (he continued on his way after helping the man).

When I visited Israel I was told the photographs from the spacecraft in the 1960s revealed, for the first time, the full scope of ancient ruins in the Middle East. These photos even included the pattern of roads leading out from the sites where cities and temples once stood. None of these features were discernable from the ground: Archaeologists have walked the terrain and examined it in detail for years without ever seeing the patterns there.

The same is true of life. When we focus too intently on our immediate situation and surroundings before surveying the whole of life's scene, we risk hitting the wrong target. We need the big picture, but then we must select our path. We then must break our journey into actionable steps that will move us forward.

Can you imagine Sir Edmund Hillary being asked how he conquered Mt. Everest and responding, "One day I went for a walk, got a bit lost and the next thing I knew I was at the top of the mountain"? Of course not! First he studied the mountain, then he developed an extensive plan, then he recruited the best guys he could find, then he accumulated the supplies, then he established a daily schedule, then he determined how long it would take – then he gave it his all. But it all started with a clear focus on where he wanted to go and how he would get there.

It is critically important that you get the best ideas that have resulted from your study of your design out of your head and onto paper. Scan the horizon to see the trends, the results, the areas that deserve your concentration. Separate priorities from that which might be distracting. And then focus on your goals one at a time, taking each successive and necessary step. Just recognize that you may have some unexpected opportunities along the way.

Vaclav Havel expressed it this way: "We must not be afraid of dreaming the seemingly impossible if we want the seemingly impossible to become a reality." There is no perfect time for which you must wait to get started. You must do more than dream. You must verbalize your priorities. You must move thoughts expressed from the lips through the fingertips. Write down your way forward, starting with your top priorities!

REFLECTION

1. Which of your life commitments is currently giving you the greatest satisfaction? Why do you think this is so?
2. What obstacles and secondary commitments are keeping you from focusing on your answer to question one? Is there anything that can be done about this?
3. What kinds of things are especially distracting to your priorities and goals? Who could help?
4. How do you think God intends for us to streamline our lives and stay focused when there are so many choices and options?
5. Read John 16:13. Give an example of how God's Spirit helped you reestablish your priorities.

CHAPTER 36

LIFE SEASONS

There are those of us who are always "about" to live. We're waiting until things change, until there is more time, until we are less tired, until we get a promotion, until we settle down — until, until, until. It always seems that there is some major event that must occur in our lives before we begin living.
— George Sheehan

The newspaper advertisement for a new car was clever. In bold type it declared the featured vehicle "goes 0-40 as fast as you did." The ad continued, "What happened? One minute you're studying for midterms, then you take a little nap and somehow wake up 20 years later with a job, a mate and a couple of kids." Frequently you hear people comment how time seems to fly by. David wrestled with this issue in Psalms 39, "Show me . . . the number of my days; let me know how fleeting is my life."

Life has its seasons. There are times when we have more energy and resources available to pursue our Divine Design than others.

Many people die before they ever really learn how to live. They put off the steps that would allow them to be fully alive and productive. Lou Erickson said that life is like a taxi. The meter keeps a-tickin' whether you are getting somewhere or standing still. Regardless of your age, there is no benefit to putting off the deployment of your Divine Design. As one seasoned beachcomber advised, "Don't stand shivering on the banks; plunge in at once and have it over with." The Bible says, "If you wait for perfect conditions you'll never get anything done."[1]

Many people spend their life as fugitives of the things they didn't do yesterday. You don't want to be one of them. So get started. But as you do, remember that life has its seasons.

If you are in early adulthood the issues of your life center around questions like: Will you be single or married? Will you have children? If yes, when and how many? Have you found a job that you love? Where are you going to live? What will you do in the community? What plan do you have for your finances? How will you spend your free time?

If you are in middle adulthood you may be asking questions about your relationship with your spouse or how to raise the kids. If you are single, you may be thinking about whether new job opportunities are worth a relocation away from friends or what causes are worth the giving of your time. Single or married, what health issues do you face? Are you taking care of aging parents? What's happening with you financially?

If you're in older adulthood your issues may surround your adult children and your grandchildren, how long you will work, what you are doing with your discretionary time, how you will face retirement, how to handle a declining network of friends.

No matter what season of life you're in, it has its unpredictable moments. Chances are, you've already had some things occur in your life that were not a part of your plan when you graduated from high school. In all my 30 years of pastoring I have yet to meet an adult who is living the exact life he or she envisioned. Many are happy about that. They are thrilled that their lives have turned out better than they had hoped. But I meet just as many people who are a long way from thanking God for their life circumstances, which have left them disappointed and in depression or despair.

It's very easy to think of your Divine Design as a set of circumstances in life when, in fact, it is the process you use to go through those circumstances. Life can be very unpredictable, and to be fully engaged in your Divine Design you must be aware of the apparent limitations of your life season. David said in Psalm 1:3 (NIV) that a successful man or woman is like a tree planted by streams of water, "which yields its fruit in season." Certain seasons are more productive. There are certain times that God appoints to us (Ecclesiastes 3:1).

We have a cluster of fruit trees in our backyard. It's frustrating to try to eat fruit in the wrong season. But when the right season comes, it seems the tree produces what's stored within effortlessly.

And could we talk about trees and fruit without mentioning pruning? In John 15:2 (NLT) Jesus says that God "cuts off every branch that doesn't produce fruit and He prunes the branches that do bear fruit so that they will produce even more." You may be in a season of your life that is for planting or producing or you may be in a season in which you are being pruned. You must remember that all the seasons are part of God's ecology.

Sometimes God cuts back certain things in your life so that you can redirect your energy. For a while you may have fewer things to do, your routines may change, and you may wonder if God has forgotten you. In certain seasons you wait. In Habakkuk 2:3 (NIV) the prophet wrote, "Though it linger, wait for it; it certainly will come." The context here is talking about the day of the Lord but the point is that God's purpose will prevail. God may be getting you ready for something or He may be getting it ready for you. Either way, it will surely come and there's no point in trying to force it before it's time.

No matter what season you pass through, you must maintain a focus on Jesus Christ at the center. Whatever is at the center of your life will be the source of your security, guidance, wisdom and power. Some people put relationships at the center, others put achievements. It is best that the center of your life be your ultimate sense of security, which cannot be taken away. Jobs can be lost, people can die, fame is fleeting. Only God stands as your strength forever.

Our attitude should be like that of the older man who was asked by a younger fellow which season of the year he liked best. "The one I'm in," was his wise reply.

REFLECTION

1. If God were to appear to you, pruning shears in hand, in what areas of your life do you think He would begin snipping? Why?
2. Describe a previous life season and the one you are in now. Compare and contrast the two.
3. Explain the meaning of this statement: "Even though your promise may be postdated, remember whose signature is on the check!"
4. Give an example of someone you have seen trying to bear fruit in the wrong season. What was the result?
5. What does Psalm 92:12 say about the righteous ones? How does this knowledge help us when we go through what appears to be a barren season?

CHAPTER 37

THE MASTER REQUIRES MASTERY

*In the confrontation between the stream and the rock, the stream always wins
– not through strength but through perseverance.*
– Unknown

Most people aren't living the life they were meant to live because they don't pursue their Divine Design.

Paganini, the great violin virtuoso, performed his first concert at age 11. He revolutionized violin technique forever. When he died in 1840, he bequeathed his violin to his birthplace of Genoa on one condition – that nobody play it ever again. The city fathers agreed and put his violin on display. But if you know anything about wooden instruments, you know that they have a certain uniqueness. So long as they're played they show no wear, but if they lie unused they begin to dry up and decay. While other instruments of the same vintage, handed down from one musician to another, continued to bless the world, Paganini's relic became a crumbling reminder of what might have been.

Where there is no gardener, there is no garden. In this case, where there is no performer, there is no performance. The apostle Paul put it this way in I Timothy 4:14 (NLT), when writing to a young leader in the church: ". . . do not neglect the spiritual gift you have received."

Gaining mastery of our gifts is certainly a lifelong process. There are several reasons we should strive for mastery. First of all, we recognize that using our gifts is a way to expand God's Kingdom. The more effective you are in discovering your Divine Design, the more you have to offer to others in service.

Secondly, as we use what we've been given, we receive more of it. The Bible says, "Give and it will be given to you. A good measure, pressed down, shaken together, and running over . . . For with the measure you use, it will be measured to you."[1]

Thirdly, there is coming an evaluation. Do you remember how, when you were in school and someone committed a serious rule violation, the teacher would threaten to record the incident on the "permanent record"? Those words still send a chill up my spine. I also remember in school asking questions like "Is this going to be on the test? Are we going to be graded on this?" Students would put more effort into something that was really going to count.

The Bible says we are creating a permanent record by the way we live. Everything we do will be graded. It's all going to be on the test. Hebrews 4:13 says that God will call every one of us into account for what we've done with our lives. God isn't using the final judgment as a manipulation tactic. His motive is to direct you to find the greatest fulfillment and joy in the pursuit of your God-given Divine Design. So He wants you to apply yourself to the task. And all of us want to stand before Him and one day hear Him say, "Well done." To hear "well done," we have to engage in repetition – to work at mastering what we have been given to do by the Master.

But what gets in the way of mastery is our comfort zones. Have you ever been to a potluck dinner where the food you eat is your own? Why? Because it's safe. You know how it's going to taste. There will be no unpleasant surprises. When you enter a room filled with people, who do you talk to first? Probably somebody you know, someone who's familiar. Someone with whom you're comfortable. But your comfort zone can imprison your progress.

> I used to have a Comfort Zone
> Where I knew I couldn't fail;
> The same four walls of busy work
> Were really more like jail.
>
> I long so much to do the things
> I'd never done before,
> But I stayed inside my Comfort Zone
> And paced the same old floor.
>
> I said it didn't matter,
> That I wasn't doing much;
> I said I didn't care for things
> Like dreams, goals and such.
>
> I claimed to be so busy
> With the things inside my zone

But deep inside I longed for
Something special of my own.
I couldn't let my life go by,
Just watching others win.
I held my breath and stepped outside
And let the change begin.

I took a step with new strength
I'd never felt before,
I kissed my Comfort Zone "good-bye"
And closed and locked the door.

If you are in a Comfort Zone,
Afraid to venture out,
Remember that all winners were
At one time filled with doubt.

A step of faith and the Word of God,
Can make your dreams come true.
Greet your future with a smile,
Success is there for you![2]

The acclaimed pianist Paderewski practiced playing musical scales for four hours a day even after he was recognized as one of the foremost musicians in the world. He is said to have told a friend that if he failed to practice for two weeks he could tell the difference in his playing. A few more weeks, he noted, the critics would notice the difference. And a few more weeks of not practicing, and the world would know that he had not practiced.

What is true with the acclaimed musician is true for all of us. Mastery is rooted in practice, and practice must continue until the very last day of this side of heaven. That does not mean that we will necessarily see results immediately. The Chinese bamboo tree is planted after the earth is prepared, and for the first four years, all of the growth is underground. The only thing visible is a little bulb and a small shoot coming out of it. Then, in the fifth year, the bamboo tree grows as high as 80 feet.

Those who seek mastery of their Divine Design understand the metaphor of the bamboo tree. They know that there is a price to be paid in preparing the ground and planting the seed and fertilizing, cultivating and watering and weeding over and over again – even when they can't see the immediate results. Ultimately they have the faith to believe that their efforts will be rewarded "far more than they would ever dare to ask or even dream of – beyond their highest prayers, desires, thoughts or hopes."[3]

REFLECTION

1. How would you respond to someone who says the gifts and talents he or she has are not worth cultivating?
2. If God grants every gift for a purpose, and we choose to neglect ours, what might be the impact on His Kingdom?
3. Imagine one day standing before the Master to give an account of the talents He's given you. What response would you expect if you had to say you were too busy to invest your talents for Him?
4. Personalize the "Comfort Zone" poem into a lesson for yourself with a specific application. Share your interpretation with a trusted friend.
5. Read Matthew 20:25 and 26. Why does Jesus make servanthood the determining characteristic of those who want to follow Him? How does this relate to mastering your Divine Design?

CHAPTER 38

FAMILY IMPLICATIONS

Childhood tendencies forecast adult abilities.
— Max Lucado

For years my wife and I were unable to have children. In desperation we contacted medical professionals, who stated that we were unlikely to conceive without a corrective operation, and even then there was no guarantee. We shared our need with our church family and asked them to pray. Thankfully, within months we were expecting the first of our three children.

During those years of infertility we made all kinds of promises to God. One was that if He would give us a child we would dedicate the child back to Him. Another was that we would do everything in our power to raise the child in His ways, not ours.

Parents who want children but don't have them tend to study families that do. We made the observation that whether parents do it purposely or not, they tend to raise children in their own image rather than encourage children to follow their own God-given identities.

Over and over again we've seen parents expecting sports prodigies receive children with artistic gifts. Or parents waiting for a child to take over the family business have a child who decides he wants to start his own. Or parents who are great with numbers and calculations receive children who'd rather spend time with animals and pets.

Wouldn't it be wonderful for adults to have a solid understanding of each child's Divine Design before they invest thousands of dollars for a college degree? Few parents pay attention to the unique strengths that are wrapped up in the package they call a son or daughter. Very often parents deliver a life plan to a child that is more a reflection of their own wishes and dreams (and in some cases, an attempt to resurrect the shattered dreams of their own life) than a reflection of God's intent.

The boxes we paint for our children are way too small. Very often parents focus on the details of the painting when they should be establishing the dimensions of the canvas. Proverbs 22:6 (MES) says, "Point your kids in the right direction – when they are old they won't be lost." There are several broad brush strokes that we should paint for our children. One includes the awareness that God cares. They need to be taught that God brought them into being and has a purpose for them that is good and fits with their creative design. When you help a child to realize that God has done this, not just for him or her but for every person on earth, and that He wants to be involved in helping those plans to be realized, you give the child a picture of his or her role and God's role in the world.

Another brush stroke to emphasize with children is that their creativity springs from God's creativity. Only God could give each person such unique talents, such different interests, such distinct characteristics. Helping a child to realize that God made funny people, numbers people, artsy people – people who can build buildings, raise good families, cure diseases – is mind boggling. To recognize that all of those beings can trace their talents and gifts to God's creative ability will give them a sense of God's power and care.

We must also help children to realize that while each of us is unique, there are some things that are the same. God wants certain things developed in all people such as godly character, Spirit-inspired wisdom, and care and compassion for others. Robin Chaddock refers to this as "a call for all."[1] It's a reminder that God is interested not just in individual success and fulfillment for ourselves, but also in faithfulness and commitment to Him, who is the source of it all.

Another brush stroke is to recognize that our Divine Design results in a divine assignment. This communicates to children that every person is important – they matter, they are unique, they are on-purpose and not accidental. Verses such as Isaiah 49:1 (NIV) reinforce this: "Before I was born the Lord called me; from my birth He has made mention of my name."

Finally we must help children recognize that they are more than just the sum of their achievements. They have value to God apart from what they do. Babies start out life by simply being. It is only later that we begin to shift the focus to accomplishment. Oswald Chambers said: "Consider the lilies of the field, how they grow . . . they simply are! Think of the sea, the air, the sun, the stars, and the moon – all of these simply are as well, yet what a ministry and service they render." Our value to God comes not from what we do for Him, but what we are to Him. We must teach children to understand that God made them so that He could love them and His greatest desire is to have them love Him back.

As parents, we have the opportunity to accelerate or squelch, to release or repress our children's Divine Design. As a parent you must be careful not to allow your children to mimic your own design or that of a sibling or peer. Each parent must understand that while a brand new baby does not come with an owner's manual, that child is preprogrammed with specific wiring. Your child's life is set on a trajectory the moment he or she is delivered to you. By age six your child has formed 85 percent of his or her personality. One of the best steps parents can take is to carefully analyze their children's God-designed itinerary. Pay close attention to what captures their imagination, what excites them, what keeps their attention, what they read, talk about, want to be a part of. "Don't see your child as a blank slate awaiting your pen, but as a written book awaiting your study."[2]

As a dad, I watched in amazement as my son showed a fascination with numbers, calculations and equations. I felt a similar surprise at my oldest daughter's compassion for the disadvantaged. Our youngest, now 21, can master a working knowledge of a foreign language in a matter of days and has already traveled around the world putting her skills to use. None of these talents can be directly traced to my wife or me. How tragic it would have been if we would have ignored or ridiculed these skills. All three have used them in selecting their life direction and vocations.

Think of the example of David in the Old Testament. Early on as a young child he displayed two strengths: fighting and music. According to I Samuel 17:34-37, he killed a lion and a bear and played a harp with great skill. Flash ahead several decades and what do we see? Two activities dominating his adult years – fighting and music. He killed tens of thousands in battle (29:5) and we still sing his songs today.

Cherish your responsibility as a parent and make an impact on your children's lives. Do so not by forcing them to construct a picture of your design but by helping them understand and appreciate and paint their own.

REFLECTION

1. Use your immediate family to give an example of two people with similar backgrounds who have very different personalities and talents. How does your family respond to each?

2. As you were growing up, where were you most nurtured (parents, God, peers, school, church)? What impact did this have on you?

3. At what point did you sense that your destiny was greater than the life direction you picked for yourself?

4. Growing up, did you feel you were valued for who you were or for what you did? Did this have any impact on your relationship with God?

5. Read Proverbs 22:6. In light of our discussions on Divine Design, explain what you think training "in the way he should go" might mean.

CHAPTER 39

IMPLICATIONS FOR YOUR WORK

I'm not here just to make a living, I'm here to make a difference.
– Helice Bridges

Laurie Beth Jones counsels employees in her book *The Path*: "If your mission does not match or closely relate to the mission statement of the place where you are employed, prepare yourself for ulcers, sleepless nights and countless hours of complaining (either by your boss, your coworkers or your stomach)."[1]

Only 17 percent of the population spends the working day doing what they really like to do. Seventy percent of people in the workplace say they have little enthusiasm or passion. Most suicides occur the night before a new work week and most heart attacks occur on Monday morning. As the astronauts used to say, "Houston, we have a problem!"

Workers in today's businesses are expecting their companies to have a deeper purpose than bottom-line profits. Even secular organizations have a heart and soul and serve a purpose in God's grand design (even if the organization and its leaders don't recognize that). Without such a foundation there will be an emptiness and hollowness that will fail to inspire workers. People today want to match their interests, passions and personalities with organizations that have the same DNA.

Your Divine Design has considerable implications for your work. So often people say they take a job to earn a lot of money so they can quit and do what they want. Don't waste time in a job that isn't an expression of your heart. Meaning is more important than money. Fredrick Buechner once stated, "The place God calls you to is the place where your deep gladness and the world's deep need meet."

Are you pursuing a career that fills you with boundless energy and passion? God intends for each of us to lovingly contribute to His world through our talents and gifts. Discovering, understanding and developing these abilities brings fulfillment and fruitfulness to your profession.

You may be employed by a company because you enjoy the good income that it provides. If your work isn't bringing you joy, are there ways to reduce your expenses so that you could begin to do work that would further express your Divine Design?

In my book *Faithspace in the Workplace*, I describe work as the intersection of your passions, gifts and goals and God's purpose. I define this as "workship." It is in this zone that we find the greatest effectiveness and efficiency. We serve God, not just our boss and our customers. Knowing our efforts have eternal value motivates us to serve with excellence. When we do, it brings glory to God and makes our work all the more satisfying.

For some reason, many people consider their vocation to be outside the realm of God's Divine Design. They see work as an obligation that they must fulfill in order to get by financially. Yet we spend most of our waking hours at work. (By the way, what you do doesn't have to come with a paycheck in order to qualify as your occupation. You may be a student or stay-at-home mom, serve in a church ministry or be a community service volunteer.) What a shame to ignore this major life investment when thinking of God's purpose for your life.

The real question, whether you literally or figuratively punch a clock, is "Do you have a clear sense that your work is an expression of what you were created and gifted to do?" Craig Groeschel states, "When you don't know the reason for a thing's existence, it is hard to avoid misusing it."[2] He tells the story of a little neighborhood girl he used to play with as a kid. One day she found a plastic, triangle-shaped object covered with holes and decided it was an oxygen mask, so she put it on her face and started to breathe through it. He didn't have the heart to tell her that it was an athletic cup. He was fairly certain, however, that if she would have known, she wouldn't have put it to such an inappropriate use!

Without understanding our God-given design and how it expresses itself through our work, we are bound to be bored, frustrated and unproductive.

Have you ever seen the painting *The Angelus* by Jean-François Millet? It portrays two peasants praying in a field. There is a church steeple on the horizon and light falling from heaven. Interestingly, the light's beam does not fall on the church or even on the bowed heads of the man and woman in the field. The rays of the sun fall on the wheelbarrow and the pitchfork at the couple's feet. The message it conveys is that God's eyes fall on the work of our hands. Mondays are as important to Him as Sundays. To Him there is no distinction between the secular and the sacred. One mom illustrates this truth with a posting on her refrigerator: "Divine tasks performed here, daily." According to the Bible your desk is your altar. Your precinct is your pulpit. Your helpfulness is your hymn.

In his book *Roaring Lambs*, Bob Briner reflected on his career and admitted that he would often find himself asking, "Why am I here?" As a Christian, he convinced himself that full-time ministry was the best way to make a difference. He later discovered that all believers are called into full-time ministry – but for most, that ministry is expressed through a career in the marketplace. "What a shame," Briner wrote, "that so many of us feel sort of in a fog between our faith and our careers. I am convinced that many Christians have no idea of the possibility of being lambs that roar – of being followers of God who know how to fully integrate their commitment to Christ into their daily lives. Maybe that's why so many areas of modern life are lacking the preserving salt of the Gospel."[3]

Do you remember when Jesus claimed Peter's boat in Luke 5? He just climbed into it and asked him to move it out from shore so that He could preach. Of course that boat represented Peter's livelihood. It's a great little reminder that all our boats belong to God. Your vessel is the place where you spend your day, where you make your living, where you live your life. Be ready for the Master to claim it! Every single day the Christ of the Bible walks among us and commandeers our truck, our classroom, our job site, our research lab to remind us that our work is really His work, and our design is really His design.

REFLECTION

1. How long were you employed before you began to sense that your job may not relate to your talents or gifts? Did you do anything about it?
2. Brainstorm a list of areas and functions within your company (or within your reach if you are unemployed) where you might have the opportunity to pursue your gifts and passions.
3. Why do you think our work is such an important place to put our Divine Design on display? What happens if we don't?

4. What is the impact on your coworkers when you use your Divine Design at work?

5. Read Hebrews 2:6-8. What are the implications of your Divine Design on the management of the earth?

CHAPTER 40

INCOME-ING

I've done so long with so little that now I can do anything with nothing.
— Unknown

When I was in college trying to figure out my future, I was given the following advice: "Find something you enjoy so much that you would do it for nothing. Then become so good at it that other people will pay you for it."

Money is not the focus of this book, just this chapter. The obvious must be stated. When we discover our Divine Design there is a much greater likelihood that we will achieve more. In our culture higher achievement is usually rewarded financially. The Bible is clear that no matter how much we make, the first part of all that we earn belongs to God. Giving Him this portion is an expression of gratitude for what He has given us and an expression of faith that He will continue to provide (including our gifts, talents and experiences that help us to earn a living in the first place).

Have you ever walked through the gaming area of a casino? You cannot ignore face after face glued to the slot machines with a set, grim, hypnotic stare as dozens rhythmically drop coins into the notorious "one-armed bandits." What a metaphor for life. So many launch into their careers with the hope that they will hit it big. But sadly their dreams are built upon cosmic luck instead of a clear plan to utilize their gifts in service to others.

If we hoard everything for ourselves, we're violating one of God's fundamental principles: "If you want something, give it away." In other words, if you want your Divine Design to be fully utilized, be generous with your resources. If you want to accomplish a dream and help other people reach their dreams, give away your time and money. Serve others with enthusiasm, and as you do, you will experience the rewards that would evade you if you sought them directly. Proverbs 11:24 (NIV) says: "There is one who scatters, yet increases more; and there is one who withholds more than is right, but it leads to poverty. The generous soul will be made rich, and he who waters will also be watered himself."

The path to fulfilling your dream is to multiply the dreams of others. When you give energy, you gain energy. When you give time, it seems like you have more. When you give knowledge away, it sharpens your own mind. When you give away your best ideas, more ideas flood into your mind. By giving, we acknowledge that the source of our supply is unending. For those pursuing their Divine Design, generosity is not an option. It's a way of life.

By faith, we declare with our actions that there are no limits because we serve a limitless God. A great example of this type of living is Joseph in the book of Genesis. Remember that he was stuck in a prison for years, unable to pursue his own dream. But while he was there he worked to make the prison run well. He supported Pharaoh's dream with his best ideas and energy. He interpreted a dream for a fellow inmate. Though initially it gained him nothing, at the proper time he was finally released and given a position of power. Ultimately he became second in command in Egypt. Joseph learned that the pathway to your dream is to help others with theirs.

While it is likely that higher returns will be achieved by those who are using their God-given uniqueness in service to others, service, not money, should be the goal. In talking with hundreds of people who have creatively used their faith to expand their service to others, it seems to be a general rule that greed is a dream blocker while generosity is a dream builder.

Acquiring and using money and resources just for our own pleasure is damaging. "If we are stingy, we'll resist the imagining and experiencing that makes us perceive others as our neighbors. We won't want to open ourselves emotionally to their needs and pleasures, lest the appeal to our minds costs us time and goods!"[1]

Dr. Paul Brand and Philip Yancey write, ". . . we are called to deny ourselves in order to open up to a more abundant life. In the exchange, the advantage clearly rests on our side: crusty selfishness peels away to reveal the love of God expressed through our own hands which, in turn, reshapes us into His image."[2] In Luke 12:15 (TNIV) Jesus cautions us: "Watch out! Be on your guard against all kinds of greed; a man's life does not consist in the abundance of his possessions." Professor Robert C. Roberts proposes that greed is a part of what he calls the "malling of our soul." He writes, "Greedy people seek out stimulations that arouse and titillate their acquisition fantasies." Just as lust looks to pornography to supply a twisted sexual gratification, "greed finds similar satisfaction in ogling stylish clothes, computers, furniture, and kitchen appliances."[3]

All of us have fallen prey to "the desire to acquire" only to realize its damaging outcome. Like the story of the poor farmer in Aesop's fable "The Goose and the Golden Egg," once we get one, we want more. But with increasing wealth comes greed and impatience. Unable to wait, day after day, for the golden eggs, the farmer decides he will kill the goose and get them all at once. But when he opens the goose, he finds it empty. There are no golden eggs – now there's no way to get any more. As we hold what we think is the wealth producer, be it our business, our skill, or our opportunity, and try to force it to produce more and more, its capacity very often expires right before our eyes. But chasing after the poisonous snake that bites us will only drive the poison through our entire system. It is better to take measures to get the poison out.

While God is not opposed to our making money or adding to our resources, these consequences should occur as a result of fulfilling our Divine Design, not in spite of it. God wants to own our hearts, but for many, money sits at the head of the table and issues its demands. Someone has said, "The average American drives his bank-financed car over a bond-financed highway on credit card gas to open a charge account at a department store so he can fill his financed home with installment-plan furniture."[4]

We must remember that everything we are and everything we have comes from someone or something else – a language, the food we eat, the structure of our thinking and yes, even our theology – all the stuff of our existence has sources other than ourselves. There is nothing original to us, and anything we create is in actuality the recombining of that which is already made. That means through parental influence, through teachers, through caregivers, workers, salespersons, we have been given all we have. It is easy to see how giving back to the height of our capacity is going to bless the world and ultimately come back to us.

God longs for us to trust Him for – and in the meantime to engage in – radical generosity. Inscribed on five of the six pillars in the Holocaust Memorial at Quincy Market in Boston are stories that speak of the cruelty and suffering in the camps. The sixth pillar presents a tale of a different sort, about a little girl named Ilse, a childhood friend of Guerda Weissman Kline, in Auschwitz. Guerda remembers that Ilse, who was about six years old at the time, found one morning a single raspberry somewhere in the camp. Ilse carried it all day long in a protected place in her pocket, and in the evening, her eyes shining with happiness, she presented it to her friend,

Guerda, on a leaf. "Imagine a world," writes Guerda, "in which your entire possession is one raspberry, and you give it to your friend."[5]

The Bible clearly directs those who would be tempted to trust riches for satisfaction to put their hope in God (I Timothy 6:17-19). When we hope in God, we can employ our Divine Design without an evaluation based on what work will earn us the most money. In Luke 12:33, 34 (NIV) Jesus describes the real bottom line: "Provide purses for yourselves that will not wear out, a treasure in heaven that will not be exhausted, where no thief comes near and no moth destroys. For where your treasure is, there your heart will be also."

It all belongs to God, both the dollars and the design.

REFLECTION

1. Every day people make job selections on the basis of salary amount. What is the impact of these decisions on the worker, the company, society, the church?

2. If you were given the opportunity to make more money by taking a new position that did not utilize any of your gifts, personality or talents, would you take it?

3. Respond to Mark Twain's statement: "You can't have everything. Where would you put it?" How can the desire to accumulate more corrupt your Divine Design?

4. Why is generosity at any level of income a prerequisite for more effective service?

5. Read the truth found in Psalm 44:3. How do our lives reflect the truth that the credit for any success or accolades we receive really belongs to God?

CHAPTER 41

THE DANGER OF BURNOUT

Experience is a hard teacher because she gives the test first, the lesson afterward.
— Vernon Sanders

The late Astronaut James Irwin said, "You might think going to the moon was the most scientific project ever. But they literally 'threw us' in the direction of the moon. We had to adjust our course every ten minutes and landed only inside 50 feet of the 500 mile radius of our target."

Discovering your Divine Design is going to require constant adjustments. In the process there is the very real possibility of experiencing emotional or physical burnout. This is especially true if you make yourself, rather than God, the center of your activities. Astronomers tell us the solar system possesses mysterious black holes whose enormous gravitational pull sucks in everything around them. When your objective is to focus on yourself rather than God's Kingdom, you experience the world as a bottomless black hole in which you never have enough. You keep pushing yourself to fill it, but you never can.

In Mark 14:38 Jesus acknowledged the fact that our spirits might be willing but our bodies are weak. In other words, there are times when the inclinations of our bodies run contrary to God's Divine Design. That's why we must constantly go to God for strength in the areas that will keep our lives in balance. Exercise, eating and drinking habits, rest, over-the-counter drugs, stress and many other issues impact our ability to finish life's race strong.

You may be like the driver who's so concerned about where he's going and how fast he can get there that he doesn't notice that the engine's knocking, the tires are losing air, the gas tank's almost empty. Then, when the car breaks down, he wonders what happened. The obvious answer is that he should have heeded the signs – and so should you.

Your Divine Design can be wrecked by the very passion and energy that fuel it if it is not managed correctly. Your pursuit is a lifelong endeavor that can't be achieved in a day or a year. It's a lifelong race, not a 100-yard dash. So we must pace ourselves for the long haul or we run the risk of burning out.

Pursuing your Divine Design is a lifelong process. Here's how Jesus put it in Matthew 11:28-30 (MES): "Are you tired? Worn out? Come to Me. Get away with Me, and you will recover your life . . . walk with Me and work with Me – watch how I do it. Learn the unforced rhythms of grace. I won't lay anything heavy or ill-fitting on you. Keep company with Me, and you will learn to live." Jesus' answer to overextension is to come to Him. It's possible to go to church and still not *come to Him*. You can read the Bible and still not *come to Him*. You can be very religious and still not *come to Him*. Yet He alone provides the solution to burnout. If you are having trouble maintaining the pace, and the strain is showing up in your family relationships, in your health, in your work, in your attitude, consider taking time out. Only you know when you need a break.

Regularly ask yourself questions such as the following:

How am I doing emotionally? Are there any emotional wounds from my past that are weighing me down?

How am I doing relationally? Are there relational wounds? Are there acts from others or wrongs (acts from me) from my past/present relationships that are weighing me down?

How am I doing physically? Are there physical weaknesses that are weighing me down?

How am I doing vocationally? Are there things at work that are weighing me down?

How am I doing mentally? Am I listening to any lies about myself that are weighing me down?

It is best to ask yourself these questions rather than to get others' evaluations. Only you know your own makeup. Others have a tendency to think they know what's best for you, but they don't. Remember, if your loved ones have to choose between having fewer things or having you, they'll always choose you. The trouble is, you may not be giving them a choice. The lifestyle you set now may be the pattern your children will follow. I've talked to many parents who regret the neglect of their children. They only recognized the consequences when their children began to neglect them.

Today is your wake-up call. Be careful not to use work as a narcotic. In our culture, hard workers are admired, but just like any other addiction, work can mask our real problem. Things will not fill the emptiness you feel inside. Only God can. Don't work so hard to buy things you don't need to impress people you don't even like.

God has made us managers, not owners, of what He has given and that includes our physical, emotional and relational lives. We are expected to take good care of what we've been given. Have you ever stopped to ask yourself why you keep pushing the accelerator to the floor – often with disastrous results? Is it envy? A need for approval? Status? Power? Riches? In one of his films, Dr. James Dobson reminds us that on the frontier, if people missed a stagecoach, they just waited another month for the next one. But today, if we miss one section of a revolving door, we have a nervous breakdown! It seems that we have more things to keep in balance and less time to do so. But you must get off the treadmill long enough to ask what is driving you. Fear of insignificance? Fear of old age, fear of loss? God can give us peace.

When I want an image of peacefulness I think of the pond near our home as I was growing up. I loved to skip stones across the quiet surface, especially disrupting the green algae that it often accumulated across its top. Even today when I skip a stone, I notice that the water does not overreact or underreact. It matches the incoming speed and the weight of the stone, distributing the force of each skip on its surface, and as the ripples fade, the water returns to a calm state (unless I jump in to retrieve the stone). No matter what crisis a stone may introduce to my relative calm, while a disruption is to be expected, I know how quickly peace can return.

Many people imagine their lives as a pie, with different pieces representing different aspects of life. There is work, family, pleasure and relationships – and then there is God's piece. But to avoid burnout, you must realize that God is not a piece – He is the whole pie, the "filling" so to speak. He holds it all together, and your Divine Design requires that He influence every piece if you hope for peace.

REFLECTION

1. What are the warning signs that you experience when your life is out of balance? Do others around you notice them too?

2. What have you discovered is the best treatment for your "burnout" symptoms? Have you ever experienced the consequence of ignoring these warning signs?

3. Is it possible to be compulsive about balancing your life? How might this disrupt your Divine Design?

4. With all the needs in the world, how do you maintain a caring heart without feeling overwhelmed?

5. Read John 14:27. Does this verse insinuate that we have control over our hearts? Does that mean that we can control anxiety, pressure and stress? If so, how are you doing?

CHAPTER 42

SEEING LIFE DIFFERENTLY

No person can make a good estimate of distant lands from the floor of the valley. A person must get to a vantage point, a viewpoint from which one can see the full breadth of the valley and gain a view of the valleys that lie beyond it.
— Unknown

A father was telling his son the Bible story about Lot. He said, "God was going to destroy the city of Sodom, so He warned Lot to take his wife and flee. But when Lot's wife looked back, she turned into a pillar of salt." Puzzled, the boy asked, "But what happened to the flea?" Tuning in to a different part of life's story makes a difference. It's all about perspective.

To see the world differently we need a paradigm shift. We need to recognize that we are not the beginning and the end, but God is. It's all about Him. When we accept His words about us and seek to understand them, it makes all the difference in the way that we live life. Consider the moon up in the night sky. One night you look up into the starry sky and see only a sliver of a moon. Another week you look up in the night sky and see perhaps a half-moon lit up, and eventually you see a full moon shining down on you. Now if you didn't know any better you'd assume that the moon shrinks and expands through the month. But because you have knowledge of astronomy you recognize that the moon remains the same size night after night. The part of the moon that is illuminated varies, but the moon remains the same. The same is true when it comes to an understanding of your Divine Design. It is a constant. The only thing that changes is your awareness of it.[1] But God wants to enlarge your perspective from seeing the personal benefits of your Divine Design to seeing how it can be used to serve Him and help others. Colossians 1:16 (TLB) expresses it well: "Christ Himself is the Creator who made everything in Heaven and in Earth, the things we can see and the things we can't; the spirit world with its kings and kingdoms, its rulers and authorities; all were made by Christ for His own use and glory. He was before all else began and it is His power that holds everything together." Your magnificence will be magnified when you get perspective!

Last year we spent a brief period of time living on the Amalfi Coast in Italy. Just above our villa was a centuries-old walkway known as Path of the Gods. It was so named because of its elevation and because it seems as though the entire southern seacoast lay beneath it. While the vistas were amazing, what fascinated me was the ability to observe the activity taking place in the town below. I learned a valuable lesson – that perspective increases as you go higher. A rock to an ant looks like a mountain, but a rock to a man looks like a rock. Who's right? It depends on your perspective.

It's been said that you can't manage what you can't measure and measurement requires a big-picture perspective. It allows you to see over the obstacles. Nietzsche said, "He who has the why to live can bear almost any how." People have been known to survive for more than an hour without oxygen. Without water, humans have lived almost a week. Without food, a few have remained alive for nearly three months. Yet without hope, without a long-term perspective, no one can survive.

Unfortunately, we get so focused on the details of life, we forget the bigger picture. Getting higher allows you to see where you want to go. Motorcyclists only pick up flyspecks when they are moving. It's good to be moving, but your windshield gets dirty. Stare at the specks on your windshield instead of the road and you will be headed for a crash. Don't spend your life staring at the flyspecks on the windows of the world. There are wonderful vistas just past them.

Get higher. See farther and more clearly. It's been said that the way to kill a man who has a great dream is to give him another one." Trying to look two places at one time is a sure way to make yourself dizzy. Paul said in Philippians 3:13 (TLB), "I am bringing all my energies to bear on this one thing . . ."

In the shadow of Saint Andrew's Cathedral in Amalfi stands a tiny paper shop. What fascinated me about the place is that it wasn't a paper outlet but a paper manufacturer. And the paper they made was the result of a painstaking process that had gone on unchanged for hundreds of years. The paper itself was quite expensive, but of course there was nothing written on it. I was reminded that what is important is not how fancy the paper might be but the content of the message written on it. Don't stare at the paper when you are supposed to be reading the message. We enter the world in relatively simple form, all looking relatively alike. But each one of us carries a message from our Creator that is, in fact, very specific and unique. Focus on the message, not its packaging.

My first attempt at a foreign language was Latin. I thought it would be easier than the other foreign languages because it's not spoken anymore. Boy was I surprised. One of the first phrases I learned in my class was "aude aliquid dignum." The phrase goes back to the sixteenth century and means "There is something worthy." While my Latin teacher used it to motivate us to learn more of the language, I think it is a good description of the importance of pursuing your Divine Design.

Listen to your life. See it for the fathomless mystery it is, and the boredom and pain of it no less than in the excitement and gladness: Touch, taste, smell your way to the holy and hidden heart of it because in the last analysis all moments are key moments, and life itself is grace.
    – Frederick Buechner

REFLECTION

1. When interviewing job candidates for the Polaroid Company, founder Edwin Land is said to have given candidates an assignment to come back the next day with three pictures that would change the world. What would your three be?

2. What is your personal process for changing your perspective when God's Spirit shows you that your current path will result in a "train disaster"?

3. Why is a specific plan so important to achieving any worthwhile goal? Share the plan you use and evaluate its effectiveness.

4. If you can't manage what you can't measure, why are many people so hesitant to take a good look at their progress (or lack thereof)?

5. Read the first part of Isaiah 37:26. Make an argument for the truth that the higher the perspective, the more you realize God is both the end and the beginning.

CHAPTER 43

OPENING THE DOOR TO OTHERS

I am done with great things and big plans, great institutions and big successes.
I am for those tiny, invisible loving human forces that work from individual to
individual, creeping through the crannies of the world like so many rootlets or
like the capillary oozing of water, yet which, if given time will rend the hard-
est monuments of human pride.
—William James

Your Divine Design will direct you into pursuits that are too big for you to do alone. Even Jesus formed a team. We must open the door to others. James 3:18 (MES) reminds us, "You can develop a healthy, robust community that lives right with God and enjoy its results only if you do the hard work of getting along with each other, treating each other with dignity and honor."

There's a legendary story about a farmer who discovered a young boy stuck in a mud bog somewhere in the United Kingdom. After much struggle, the farmer was finally able to free the lad, although for a moment the farmer felt that he, too, would sink too deeply into the mud to survive. Later that evening a lord stopped by the farmer's humble shanty, identifying himself as the rescued boy's father and offering to pay him a generous reward for his effort.

When the farmer refused, the lord saw that the farmer had a son and insisted that he pay the boy's way to college. After he graduated with a degree in science, the young man – Alexander Fleming – went on to discover penicillin. Ironically, the young man who had been rescued from the bog, now a young adult, came down with pneumonia. Thanks to Fleming's discovery, his life was saved. The young man's name was Sir Winston Churchill.[1] The point is, we cannot survive without others. We all have something to contribute and what we contribute very often comes back to us multiplied.

To succeed, we all need a relational support system. These partners in giftedness help remind us that we cannot go it alone. What a relief it is to find that one individual does not need to be gifted in all ways a certain life situation demands. Others can fill in the gaps and help us. Two people working together can accomplish so much more than one alone. Yet we live in a society that seems to advocate self-sufficiency. The father of modern stress research, Hans Selye, compares the independent achievement focus to "the development of a cancer, whose most characteristic feature is that it cares only for itself. Hence, it feeds on the other parts of its own host until it kills the host – and thus commits biological suicide, so that the cancer cell cannot live except within the body in which it started its reckless, ego-centric development."[2]

When a new highway loop was being completed in West Michigan, a real danger was discovered. The bridges had been designed to bear their own weight – but not the traffic they were intended to carry. Before the highway could be opened the bridges had to be reengineered and rebuilt. Sadly, many people engineer their lives with a design that bears only their own weight and cannot carry anyone else. As a result, their life pathways are closed to others. What a sad waste of potential.

What happens when we work together to communicate a "we" story instead of a "me" story?

1. We accomplish more
2. We generate more energy
3. We show that we value others
4. We help each other become more successful

Detail thinkers need global thinkers. Introverts need extroverts. We all need each other.

One of my granddaughter's favorite stories is that of Cinderella. She especially enjoys the part of the story where everyone tries to stuff their oversized foot into a glass slipper that was exclusively designed for the main character.

The person who tries to fill a job when he or she is not gifted for it reminds me of those who are Cinderella wannabes. Only God is all-purpose. No person is. And the challenge for each of us is to find and then work in close proximity with those who complement our talents and gifts. Relationships reflect God's heart. When He created the world He said that everything was good except the fact that man was alone.

God wants us to experience His fullness through great relationships. Recognizing our need of others is a great first step. Ecclesiastes 4:9 and 10 (NIV) says, "Two are better than one because they have a good return for their work; if one falls down, his friend can help him up. But pity the man who falls and has no one to help him up!" We are so used to being independent and doing things on our own. Most of us prefer to drive solo. But, you need to ask, who represents the missing pieces you need? Who does God want in your life to help you achieve your God-given design?

While not everyone is known for a high IQ or creative or artistic skill, every person has a place where he or she has the highest capacity for effective service in the world. We recently had our church property appraised and there was a whole section in the appraisal devoted to what, in real estate, they call "best use." For example, my "best use" is in leading and speaking. My engines "rev" when I am involved in those activities and God seems to bless my efforts. People have come to me for counseling and later told me that my insights and encouragement helped. But I have to tell you that when they walked out the door after the session I felt exhausted, not energized. And when it comes to counseling, after a couple of sessions, I just want to tell people, "Okay, now you know what the problem is, so start doing the right thing and don't do the wrong thing. Thanks for coming. God bless you." While some may consider me a good counselor, I would never say counseling is a "best use" for me. On the other hand, we have people in our church who love to take people by the hand and graciously lead them to the next step and patiently wait for them to respond. These gifts are needed and are very different than mine.

We all have areas where we shine and areas where we're weak and that is why it is only *together* that we make up the body of Christ. I Corinthians 12:6-8 says, ". . . God Himself is behind it all. Each person is given something to do that shows who God is: Everyone gets in on it, everyone benefits. All kinds of things are handed out by the Spirit, and to all kinds of people! The variety is wonderful . . ."

To fulfill your Divine Design you've got to invest in those relationships. Give yourself away. Ecclesiastes 11:1 says, "Cast your bread on the water, and it will come back to you." Love as if your love is unlimited. Remember, caring and relating to others is a checking account, not a savings account. Keep writing checks of support, encouragement, charity and love and you'll find that the more of it you give away, the more you get in return. One of the ways that you invest in those relationships is to "serve one another in love." By helping others you will receive help in return. And together you not only fulfill your Divine Design, but help others to do the same.

REFLECTION

1. Who has had the greatest spiritual impact on you? Do you think this was the result of their understanding of their own Divine Design? Explain.

2. You are just one part of the body of Christ. Identify two or three other parts and explain how you all fit together.

3. List three of your closest friends. In what area are they a "10"?

4. If you had a God-given label under the heading "Best Use," what would be on it?

5. Read Ephesians 4:7 and 16. What is the relationship between love and discovering and developing your Divine Design? How does this work?

CHAPTER 44

THE NEXT STEP

It's fine to build castles in the air, so long as you work to put foundations under them.
— Henry David Thoreau

Oswald Chambers said, "Dreaming about a thing in order to do it properly is right; but dreaming about it when we should be doing it is wrong."

Now that you more fully understand your Divine Design, are you willing to act on it? The timing couldn't be more perfect. Chances are you will never have more information about your unique design than you have now. What will you do with it? Don't let your Divine Design die of neglect. Wishing and hoping and thinking and dreaming of your Divine Design won't bring your goals any closer. But planning for it will. The Bible expresses it this way:

> Set up road signs;
> > put up guideposts.
> Take note of the highway,
> > the road that you take.
> > — Jeremiah 31:21

Many people dream about living differently, but few have the courage to face the discomfort necessary to make a change. The crew of a 747 can sit at the end of the runway all day long, knowing the plane is free to take off. They may have received clearance from the tower again and again. They also know that the power in the engines is available. But the plane will never get off the ground until the controls are activated. The plane must be in a moving position. If faith without works is dead (James 2:20), then a Divine Design without determination to act is dead too. Unfortunately, too many goals drown in the sea of good intentions.

One retired NFL offensive lineman said that the toughest thing about staying in shape for a professional athlete is walking through the front doors of the gym. So that's all he focuses on – getting to the gym. Once he's there, good conditioning follows. You must get yourself to the gym, or do whatever is the next step for you. Nothing will torpedo your dreams faster than a lack of action.

Don't wait for complete understanding of every detail of your design before starting the process. Erwin McManus, in his book *Seizing Your Divine Moment*, says: "Don't look for God to fill in all the blanks. Don't wait for Him to remove all the uncertainty. Realize He may actually increase the uncertainty and leverage all the odds against you, just so you will know in the end that it wasn't your gifts but His power, through your gifts, that fulfilled His purpose in your life.[1]

What dream has God been bringing to the surface over your weeks of study? What have you been in-"visioning" that doesn't yet exist? Remember Paul's words in Ephesians 3:20 (MES): "God can do . . . far more than you could ever imagine or guess or request in your wildest dreams!"

William Carey was ridiculed by many because he had his "head in the clouds." He studied foreign languages and the travel logs of Captain Cook. While just a cobbler he kept a huge map on the wall of his workshop so that he could pray for the nations every day. One night after he had spoken at a conference on the subject, *Is the Great Commission for Today?* an older minister got up and publicly rebuked him, saying, "If God wants to convert the heathen, he'll do it without your help or mine." The older minister won the battle that night, but Carey won the war. Before he died he took the Gospel to India and is widely regarded the Father of Modern Missions!

Baseball Hall of Famer Yogi Berra declared, "The future isn't what it used to be." Although that may be true, it's still the only place we have to go. Your potential lies ahead of you – whether you're 12, 32, 52 or 82. There are still opportunities to grow and challenges to meet. As the Spanish proverb says, "He who does not look ahead remains behind."

It is important to realize that when you begin to pursue your Divine Design, things won't always go smoothly. Others may ridicule it, become threatened by it or refuse to support it. But each day you don't act, a part of your dream will die. The way to overcome this is to ask yourself, "What is the next thing I need to do to fulfill my Divine Design?" Overwhelming assignments can be overcome by just taking one step at a time. Most people want God to act before they take a step of faith, but you must act on faith first. Faith means believing God more than our five senses. You may think that's too hard, but you can do it. The Bible says in Romans 12:3 that every person has a measure of faith. We simply need to use the faith we have.

This is the fifth book I've written (the third to be published), yet every time I go through the process it overwhelms me. I scour at least 75 volumes before beginning to write. That takes me hundreds of hours before I ever put a pen to paper. And of course the rest of my life can't be put on hold.

Many times throughout the process I freeze up. I have learned to break out of this dilemma with a very simple process. I pray to God, who is my inspiration, and I ask myself, "What is the very next step?" The very next step may be as simple as looking up the source of a quote or as challenging as developing the basic outline. But I force myself to keep moving forward.

How can you move forward? Now that you have considered your beliefs, convictions, vision, strengths and dreams, you can begin to determine how you will fulfill what God is calling you to do. Ask yourself, "What is my next step?"

- It might be making a phone call to someone doing what you want to do
- It might be uttering a prayer
- It might be collecting some resources or consulting with a church leader
- It might be talking to your boss about a new assignment

Whatever it is, pray to God and then just do it. Keep the wheel turning. Keep the ball moving. Keep the body in motion. Herbert Spencer said, "A living thing is distinguished from a dead thing by the multiplicity of the changes at any moment taking place in it." Think of the centipede. With all those legs moving a millimeter at a time, you'd think he wouldn't get anywhere. But take your eye off him for a moment and he's gone. All of your small steps can result in surprising progress.

Action is evidence of life. You cannot accomplish your Divine Design without change. And change requires movement. You cannot become what you were destined to be by remaining what you are. You can't fulfill your Divine destiny without work. None of the steps to success that we've discussed so far will work unless you do.

REFLECTION

1. What next step would you focus on if you knew there was no possibility of failure?
2. Look around your home, your office or any place you spend time and notice the types of things in your surroundings. What clues do these things give to your life focus? How do they help you formulate your next step?
3. Forward progress requires a next step. When walking, the next step saves us from collapsing. Describe the danger that may be lurking if you do not take the next step in your Divine Design.
4. Have you ever had to change course in a major area of your life because you "hit a wall"? How do you generate momentum again?
5. Why is Ephesians 2:8 and 9 a good caution to remember when setting up a plan for your next steps?

CHAPTER 45

CHARACTER MATTERS

We never know how high we are
Til we are called to rise.
And then, if we are true to plan
Our statures touch the skies.
— Emily Dickinson

The lives of many are rendered ineffective because of character. Character is the delivery system for our talent and abilities. To paraphrase Emerson, "What you are shouts so loudly I can't appreciate what you do." It is difficult to benefit from the service of others when it is apparent the service has been corrupted through a weak or unstable character. In the words of William George Jordan, "Into the hands of every individual is given a marvelous power for good or evil – the silent, unconscious, unseen influence of his life. This is simply the constant radiation of what man really is, not what he pretends to be."

It is difficult to separate character from our habits. I taught each of my children this profound truth: "Sow a thought, reap an action; sow an action, reap a habit; sow a habit, reap a character; sow a character, reap a destiny." The great educator Horace Mann once said, "Habits are like a cable. We weave a strand of it every day and soon it cannot be broken."

The 1986 movie *Hoosiers* is one of the great sports movies of all time. Gene Hackman plays Coach Norman Dale, who comes to a small Indiana town with a checkered past. His goal is to bring out the best of a small group of young men who form the 1954 Hickory High School basketball team.

Dale ruffles feathers when he insists that the boys focus on the fundamentals of the game such as conditioning, dribbling, defense, passing and teamwork. This is a tough adjustment because the boys have been focused on the shooting talent of one star by the name of Jimmy. The townspeople who love the team side with Jimmy because they know that shooting the ball is the only way to win the game.

So why focus on fundamentals? Coach Dale explains that the fundamentals help the team keep their wits about them when faced with adversity. Fundamentals build a strong foundation that helps the team stay disciplined and focused, laying the base for our true and sometimes hidden talent to shine.

According to the Bible, tending to the basics helps us develop a pure heart. Matthew 5:8 says the pure in heart shall see God. It's impossible to get a crystal clear perspective on our divine assignment without focusing on what is fundamental. Micah 6:8 (NIV) states: "And what does the Lord require of you? To act justly and to love mercy and to walk humbly with your God."

No one will give you more trouble than yourself. Oliver Wendell Holmes stated, "What lies behind us and what lies before us are tiny matters compared to what lies within us." The first and best victory is to conquer yourself. You can't change the fruit until you change the root. It all starts with God and it is part of everyone's personal divine assignment. Richard N. Bolles makes this point in his book *What Color Is Your Parachute?* He's a deeply devoted Christian and describes our need to develop our relationship with God and others as a mission that is "one which you share with the rest of the human race, but is no less your individual Mission for that fact that it is shared."[1]

In Matthew 22:37-39 (NIV), when Jesus was asked what are the most critical factors to living a productive life, He quoted from the Old Testament: "Love the Lord your God with all your heart and with all your soul and with all your mind . . . and the second is like it: Love your neighbor as yourself."

So the fundamentals in the development of our character, according to Jesus, include first of all loving God wholeheartedly. Without developing our relationship with Him we can become apathetic or fearful or hopeless. The Bible says that we grow in our love of God by receiving and responding to His love of us. Any relationship requires communication. God has communicated to us through the Bible and we respond to Him in prayer. This dialogue, in turn, strengthens our relationships.

Secondly, we have a responsibility to love ourselves. As the airlines would say, you need to put on your own oxygen mask before trying to help those around you. This doesn't mean it's all about me. It simply means that an awareness of God's love of me is going to result in a healthy self-love and that is fundamental to my capacity to love others or let God love others through me. When we talk about our Divine Design and the purpose that God has for each of us, we have a tendency to focus on being "used by

God." But it is quite possible that that is how we'll end up feeling – used. God doesn't want us to be His puppets, but His partners. When we understand God's love of us, we are more likely to have a healthy perspective about our place in the world.

Also, our associations matter. Any parent would assert that one of the most important decisions made by children is choosing friends. We must be careful to avoid being influenced by those who do not respect or hold to our values. Centuries ago, the slave Aesop penned a fable about a mouse who always lived on the land. By an unlucky chance, this mouse formed an intimate acquaintance with a frog who lived, for the most part, in the water.

One day the frog (why do frogs get all the best stories?) was intent on mischief. He tied the foot of the mouse tightly to his own. With the two joined together, the frog led his friend to the meadow where they usually searched for food. Gradually, the frog led the mouse toward the pond in which he lived. When he reached the banks of the water he suddenly jumped in, dragging the mouse with him.

Enjoying the water immensely, the frog swam, croaking about as if he had done a good deed. The desperate mouse soon sputtered and drowned, his poor dead body floating about on the surface.

A hawk observed the floating mouse from the sky and dived down and grabbed it with his talons, carrying it back to his nest. The frog, still fastened to the leg of the mouse, was also carried off a prisoner and was eaten by the hawk. Of course, the moral is to choose your associations wisely. The wrong person may lead you down the wrong path and into the wrong pond. Those of us who don't have the strength to swim will inevitably drown.

Character traits are typically seen in what you say and how you act. They include both inner (emotional, spiritual) and outer (physical, behavioral) qualities. And when it comes to your Divine Design, character matters.

Reflection

1. Sometimes we can get to the heart of our motivations by asking ourselves the "why" question. By now you have some understanding of your Divine Design. Project a one-year plan to implement it. Then ask yourself the why question five consecutive times as to why you think this is a good plan, giving a different answer each time. Why? Why? Why? Why? Why?

2. List what you consider to be five essential "fundamentals" of life and the age that you learned them. Explain why you believe each is critically important.

3. Explain this statement: "The first and best victory is to conquer yourself." Give an example of ignoring this wisdom.

4. What role do our friends and close associates play in our character development? Assign a letter grade (A-F) to how your current friends are impacting your character.

5. Read James 2:14, 17 and 18. How do a person's actions reveal his or her true character? When you discover a character weakness in yourself, what do you do so that it doesn't negatively influence those you want to reach for Christ?

CHAPTER 46

TRACKING THE DESIGN TO THE DESIGNER

This is the true joy in life, the being used for a purpose recognized by yourself as a mighty one . . . the being a force of nature instead of a feverish, selfish little clod of ailments and grievances complaining that the world will not devote itself to making you happy.
— George Bernard Shaw

A quick reading of contemporary literature would lead one to conclude that human beings are either animals or gods, or some combination of both. The problem is, larger things cannot be derived from smaller. And complex things cannot be derived from primitive. What a leap of faith it would require for us to imagine that the beauty of our design has its ultimate origin in a primordial mud of evolutionary theory. That is a leap that few intellectually honest people can make.

If God is the prime designer, then whoever He is cannot be less than what He designed. Carlos Corretto said, "We are the wire, God is the current. Our only power is to let the current pass through us." A careful look at the genius involved in the creation of nature or of the cosmos or of a human personality presents us with a reasonable assumption that God is personal. He has a plan for what He created.

Remember playing treasure hunt as a child? It's a pirate game that you might have enjoyed at a birthday party or with a friend, exploring a beach or a playground or a path through the woods. Maybe you searched for treasure in someone's attic or looked for hidden prizes in a friend's basement as he or she guided you with terms such as "warm" or "cold." The search for hidden treasure is a part of nearly everyone's experience. It's one of the oldest of stories – searching for a prize, for a lost kingdom or something of great worth in an unlikely place. It's a favorite theme of fairy tales and legends. And the magic of the story is that treasures really do exist. But what makes the story so much fun is that the treasures are hidden. You come across something that's been there all the time, but you either overlooked it or didn't know where to hunt for it.

The modern fable by Pablo Coehlo called *The Alchemist* tells a story of a character who learns that the key to happiness is following his heart. By doing so, he will fulfill his personal legend and find his "treasure." According to the story, each of us has a legend that is distinctly ours. Our heart provides us with clues, but most of us ignore them and we therefore fail to live our legend. Instead, we let our lives wander in no apparent direction, toward no apparent end. We die, as Oliver Wendell Holmes observed, with our music still inside us.[1]

You have a whole treasure chest full of resources, a deep storage of unexplored possibilities of hidden strengths and unknown powers. And when you begin to identify them and draw on them and help others with them, the logical question to ask is "Who put them there in the first place?"

Think of it in terms of natural resources. Thousands of years ago this planet had all the gold, silver, oil and diamonds that it has now. But before we identified oil or coal or diamonds as resources, we didn't know we had them. But they were there all along. Did they get there by accident? Unlikely. We can track these resources to the resource Provider.

We do not have the resources necessary within ourselves to become anything we want to become. Our Divine Designs are a divine gift. And the only way to properly use them is to offer them back to God through surrender and worship. After all, the end of a God-inspired Divine Design is God Himself. We must remember that the goal is not the design itself but the Designer. Psalm 89:6 reminds us, "To what can we compare God? Who in the skies is comparable to the Lord? Who among the sons of the mighty is like the Lord?"

Max Lucado suggests, "What you are to a paper airplane, God is to you. Take a sheet of paper and make one. Contrast yourself with your creation. Challenge it to a spelling contest. Who will win? Dare it to race you around the block. Who is faster? Invite the airplane to a game of one-on-one basketball. Will you not dominate the court? And well you should. The thing has no brainwaves, no pulse. It exists only because you formed it and it flies only when someone throws it. Multiply the contrast between you and the paper plane by infinity and you will begin to catch a glimpse of the disparity between God and us."[2]

The Bible puts it this way in Isaiah 46:9-11 (NLT): "I am God – I alone! I am God, and there is no one else like Me. Only I can tell you what's going to happen even before it happens. Everything I plan will come to pass, for I do whatever I wish . . . I have said I would do it, and I will."

As I write these words, Billy Graham's wife, Ruth, has just passed away. He is in poor health himself. Having personally preached to more than 200 million people, Dr. Graham reflected on his achievements:

> I have often said that the first thing that I'm going to do when I get to Heaven is to ask, "Why me, Lord? Why did you choose a farm boy from North Carolina to reach so many people, to have such a wonderful team of associates and to have a part in what You were doing in the later half of the 20th century?"

> As I look back over the years, however, I know that my deepest feeling is one of overwhelming gratitude. I cannot take credit for whatever God has chosen to accomplish through us and our ministry; only God deserves the glory and we can never thank Him enough for the great things He has done.[3]

No matter how much you discover of your God-designed design, you always end up asking yourself the question "Why me?" The Bible answers the question clearly: because of His love. God loves you deeply, passionately, unconditionally, and eternally. No other truth can heal your restless psyche, your bruised ego, your shattered dreams, or your inappropriate opinions of yourself. This truth is necessary to believe before we can understand and live our Divine Design. Once you embrace it you'll see its thread weaving through your life, into and out of activities, across experiences, and through the years.

We all have these threads that give us clues to our Divine Design. Sometimes they are on the surface and sometimes they are woven deep in our fabric, waiting to reemerge at a later time. Capture these threads and use them to create a beautiful life. Avoid allowing them to be torn and frayed, or worse, losing sight of them altogether. Your Divine Design is a beautifully crafted embroidery, but perhaps you are looking at its underside. One day you will see how wisely and perfectly the Designer has woven the threads of your design together.

REFLECTION

1. In the progression of this study, what has a deeper look at your own design taught you about the Designer?
2. How has your awareness of the treasure placed within you deepened your worship life?
3. Describe how using your Divine Design for your own benefit and not for God's is actually a form of idolatry.
4. How can a rejection of your Divine Design be seen as a rejection of God Himself?
5. Read Matthew 6:21. Using this verse, explain how hidden treasures that relate to your Divine Design may be found in the heart.

CHAPTER 47

COMPLETE SURRENDER

The more we get what we now call "ourselves" out of the way and let Him take us over, the more truly ourselves we become.
— C. S. Lewis

And so, we're back to where we started. Each of us is a spiritual, emotional, mental, relational, and physical being. Western civilization tends to isolate those areas of our lives but we are integrated beings. You cannot talk about your spiritual life without describing what you feel and think. You are "one." Each aspect of your creation is related to all the others.

Like a multifaceted diamond there are different sides to your being, each radiating a degree of life, but all are part of the same stone. It is your spirit that ultimately drives the different facets of your life. When that spirit is self-absorbed, all thoughts and emotions relate to pleasing and advancing yourself. But when the spirit is turned to God and empowered by His Spirit, you are turned inside out. The Bible calls this becoming a "new creature." Your responses, goals, thoughts, and desires undergo radical transformation as your life in Christ deepens and you increasingly surrender to Him. Jesus said in Luke 14:33, "Any of you who does not give up everything he has cannot be My disciple."

Every desire you have is not necessarily sourced in your Divine Design. There are times when you may pursue a creative idea to the exclusion of your Creator. Larry Crabb puts it this way: "The existence of a desire does not justify its satisfaction." Everything we hope, dream and wish for is not God's to satisfy but is ours to surrender.

If you've ever studied music, you know that nearly every symphony has a leitmotif – a set of notes that form a dominant theme that repeats itself in various forms throughout each of the symphony's movements. For the Christian, this is Christ. He is the theme in every area of our lives. While the choice to pursue our Divine Design may be up to us, the real work of accomplishing it is God's. It is His power that works in us (II Corinthians 12:9), but it is our work to be faithfully devoted to Him.

A budding artist once came to writer Leo Tolstoy to show him his just-completed painting of the Last Supper and asked, "What do you think?" Tolstoy quietly studied the picture. He pondered every detail as the artist waited impatiently. The silence was finally broken as Tolstoy slowly pointed to the central figure. "You don't really love Him," he said quietly. The confused young man responded, "Why, that is the Lord Jesus Christ!"

"I know," said Tolstoy, "but if you loved Him more, you would have painted Him better." While most of us aren't budding artists, we are budding servants and the quality of our love for Christ is seen in the brush strokes of our service to Him and others.

We must empty ourselves. Full containers can't be filled. A clenched fist can't receive anything. Instead of hoarding our hours we should give generous service to others. Instead of being tight-fisted with our money, we should hunt down opportunities to underwrite a person or ministry that needs it. God will see to it that you never lack resources for any good work (II Corinthians 9:8) if you completely commit yourself to Him.

W. H. Murray in the *Scottish Himalayan Expedition* wrote: "Until one is committed there is hesitancy, the chance to draw back, always ineffectiveness. Concerning all acts of initiative (and creation) there is one elementary truth, the ignorance of which kills countless ideas and splendid plans: the moment one definitely commits oneself, then providence moves too. All sorts of things occur to help one that would otherwise never have occurred. A whole stream of events issues from the decision, raising in one's favor all manner of unforeseen incidences and meetings and material assistance, which no man could have dreamed would have come his way."[1]

So how do we more completely surrender? Certainly developing spiritual disciplines are important. Bible study, worship, fellowship with other believers, accountability, service, giving and outreach are basic ingredients for a life lived close to God's heart. But we even approach these disciplines in ways that follow our Divine Design.

When my son was growing up we would experience life by playing sports together. My oldest daughter and I would experience life as we would go on our Friday luncheon dates and she would talk and talk and I would listen and listen. My youngest daughter and I often experience life by journaling. Especially when we travel, we will document the events we experience and then compare our writings.

How can we experience life with the One who loves us – our Creator? Practice the ways that work for you. Those ways may change as you pass through different seasons of your life, but they will still be unique to you. As Max Lucado says, "Don't go to God with options and expect Him to choose one of your preferences. Go to Him with empty hands – no hidden agendas, no crossed fingers, nothing behind your back. Go to Him with a willingness to do whatever He says. If you surrender your will, then He will 'equip you with everything good for doing His will.' "[2]

Here's an example. I have adapted the widely circulated letter from Bob Morehead, a young African follower of Jesus Christ, for an example of the depth of surrender we are talking about. He states:

> I am part of the "Church for all Ages."
>
> The die has been cast. I have stepped over the line.
> The decision has been made. I will relentlessly follow.
>
> I won't look back, let up, slow down, back away, or be still.
> My past is forgiven, my present has purpose, and my future is secure.
>
> I am finished with sensual living, shallow conversations, filling the expectations of others, timid dreams, miserly giving, and selfish goals.
>
> I no longer need preeminence, prosperity, position, promotions, platitudes, or popularity.
>
> I now live in God's presence, grow by faith, love by passion, live by patient prayer, labor by His power.
>
> My pace is set, my gait is fast, my goal is God's glory, my road is narrow, my way is rough, my companions few, my God reliable, my mission clear.
>
> I cannot be bought, compromised, deterred, lured away, turned back, diluted, or delayed.

I will not flinch in the face of sacrifice, hesitate in the presence of adversity, negotiate at the table of the enemy, ponder at the pool of popularity, or meander in the maze of mediocrity.
My salvation has made me a slave of my Redeemer.

I must work until He returns, give until I'm empty, share until all know, then start all over again.

And when He comes to get His own, He will have no problem recognizing me. My allegiance will be clear.[3]

Take your everyday, ordinary life – your sleeping, eating, going-to-work, and walking-around life – and place it before God as an offering.
– Romans 12:1 (MES)

REFLECTION

1. When all the pieces of a design fit well and operate smoothly, it may be said to have structural integrity. Do you see ways in which your personal Divine Design has integrity? Explain.
2. What role does "committing" to your Divine Design have in relation to its efficiency? Describe a time when you failed to make the commitment. What was the result?
3. Describe a time in your life when you served out of love and a time when you did not. How did each make you feel?
4. Do you agree or disagree with the statement "If you loved Him more, you would serve Him better"? Explain.
5. Read II Corinthians 5:20. As ambassadors we have a single priority – to represent our King. Explain how a misunderstanding or misappropriation of our Divine Design can thwart our role as ambassadors.

\

CHAPTER 48

THE ROLE OF THE LOCAL CHURCH

There are no "little people" in the body of Christ, and there are no "insignificant" ministries.
— Rick Warren

According to the Bible, every believer is called into ministry – ministry in the church and ministry in the world. While we often call a pastor of a church "a minister," the Bible says each of us is called to that role.[1] Your Divine Design is made for ministry. Ministry is simply serving others in Christ's name. While some ministries are very visible and others are behind the scenes, they are all important. Just like every believer is interconnected with every other, so is every ministry related to all the others. Since no single person or single ministry can accomplish all that God intends, we must depend on and cooperate with each other.

Obviously God would not give us inborn abilities, talents, personalities, spiritual gifts and experiences and then not use them. God expects your Divine Design to be expressed through the church. Ephesians 1:5 (NLT) states: "His unchanging plan has always been to adopt us into His own family by bringing us to Himself through Jesus Christ. And this gave Him great pleasure."

When you place your trust in Jesus Christ, He intends for you to be specifically connected to other believers in a local church. The church, God's family, has an eternal life span. I Timothy 3:15 (GW) says, "God's family is the church of the living God, the pillar and foundation of the truth." Some of God's greatest gifts to us are our brothers and sisters in Christ. Five years ago my life was out of control. Our church had grown from 20 to 2,000 and I had several dozen direct reports. We were in the middle of a $10 million building project and as I strolled the construction site I remember thinking that with all the stress I wonder if I'll be still standing at its completion. Carl George, a nationally recognized church consultant, happened to be in the area and stopped by. He put me in touch with a friend of his by the name of chuck faber (no that isn't a typo; he prefers his name spelled with lowercase letters) who was in another church and was looking to make a change. chuck and I began an e-mail correspondence that would fill several volumes. chuck just *happened* to have the exact bundle of gifts that our church needed at the time. He helped restore my joy in ministry and has become not only my dedicated associate, but my dearest friend. In fact, the very reason I can spend this time writing, and hopefully you can benefit, is because of chuck. You see, God's work gets amplified when chuck and I put our gifts together. And then when those gifts are combined with those of Kathy and Sally and Mike and Dave and Robin and Chris . . . well, you get the picture.

When we work together, each of us functioning in the context of our Divine Design and looking to God to provide His power and wisdom, we become unstoppable. We become a winning team that can score points for God's Kingdom. In II Corinthians 10:13 (TLB) Paul put it this way: "We will not boast of authority we do not have. Our goal is to measure up to God's plan for us."

We can't do everything, but we can do some things within the realm of our Divine Design incredibly well. And we do it better when we stay in an environment that can nurture us spiritually. God wants us incubated in the hothouse of a church filled with people who are committed to His ways and His Word. So why do we find so many churchgoers who begin to cool and drift?

When our children were young and we would take them to the beach, we would always begin every trip by educating the youngest among us about the undertow. The pull of the current can cause us to drift without realizing it. So we teach them to identify a location on the shore and then to keep themselves aligned with it. It becomes their point of reference. Many people in the church look as though they have vital relationships with God, but inwardly their hearts have drifted. They've gotten off track and they need to be realigned.

We have the potential to work together by pooling our strengths in a way that makes our weaknesses irrelevant. Did you know that approximately 147 million Americans are incapable of seeing with 20/20 vision? Seven hundred years ago anyone cursed with farsightedness, shortsightedness, or astigmatism would have been seriously handicapped. But as the science of optics developed, it became possible to grind lenses that would correct for these conditions. These lenses were then mounted in frames to make glasses. And with this one invention, the weakness of the imperfect vision was reduced to an irrelevant non-talent. Millions of Americans still suffer with imperfect vision, but armed with the support system of glasses or contact lenses, it makes no difference. The speediest cure for a debilitating weakness is a support system.[2] And the greatest way to maximize a talent is to place it in the context of others who appreciate it. That should be the local church!

The apostle Paul made this point in I Corinthians 12:14-18 (MES) when he used the human body as an analogy to the body of Christ. He states that every part is important. "It's all the different-but-similar parts arranged and functioning together. If Foot said, 'I'm not elegant like Hand, embellished with rings; I guess I don't belong to this body,' would that make it so? If Ear said, 'I'm not beautiful like Eye, limpid and expressive; I don't deserve a place on the head,' would you want to remove it from the body? If the body was all Eye, how could it hear? If all Ear, how could it smell? As it is, we see that God has carefully placed each part of the body right where He wanted it."

When does the body function most effectively? When it's all there; when every member is there doing what it's supposed to do. When the hands are being hands and the feet are being feet and the ears are being ears and all of them work together for the same common goal. This brings balance to the church, and lasting spiritual growth can take place in a way that makes a maximum impact on the world.

Church leaders are responsible to open the doors of service for the members of their congregations, and the focus should be on empowering people, not filling positions. Find and become a part of a church that places a high value on helping you discover, develop and deploy your gifts in ministry. Martin Luther King, Jr., expressed it well: "Everybody can be great . . . because anybody can serve. You don't have to have a college degree to serve. You don't have to make your subject and verb agree to serve, you only need a heart full of grace. A soul generated by love."

Serving together, using our combined gifts and abilities, demonstrates to the world the beauty and power of the body of Christ.

REFLECTION

1. Describe how what might be called "behind the scenes" serving has personally helped you. How might your life be different if those with these gifts hadn't taken their role seriously?

2. Why is the church a great laboratory for experimenting with our Divine Design?

3. What should people do if they find that their role at their local church is not a "fit"?

4. The apostle Paul was happiest when the church was like-minded, serving with one spirit and purpose (Philippians 2:2). Why do you think this goal was so important to him? How would you rate your church in this area?

5. Read Luke 5:18-20. Discuss the lessons this story contains for a ministry done together rather than alone.

CHAPTER 49

A KINGDOM FORCE

Do all the good you can, by all the means you can, in all the ways you can, in
all the places you can, at all the times you can, with all the people you can,
as long as ever you can.
— John Wesley

While the church is the vehicle of our Divine Design, the Kingdom of God is the objective. Max Lucado tells the story of a Bible class teacher he remembers from his childhood. She gave each of her students a can of crayons and a sketch of Jesus torn from a coloring book. " 'Take the crayons I gave you,' she would instruct, 'and color Jesus.' " He recalls, "We didn't illustrate pictures of ourselves; we colored the Son of God. We didn't pirate crayons from other cans; we used the ones she gave us. This was the fun of it. 'Do the best you can with the can you get.' No blue for the sky? Make it purple. If Jesus' hair is blond instead of brown, the teacher won't mind. She loaded the can."[1] How could children be blamed for creating their works of art with only the colors they were given? The author makes the point that the teacher taught the class to paint Jesus with their own colors.

That is what God does for us — loads our can, gives us a unique set of colors and then asks us to use them to illustrate Christ. We draw attention to Him through our creations. No matter where we start on the picture, He is the image we're drawing. When we show Him to our unchurched friends, relatives and coworkers, we extend His rule on the earth and expand His Kingdom.

As Paul wrote in I Corinthians 13:12 (RSV/NIV), "Now we see in a mirror, dimly, but then face to face. Now I know in part, but then I shall know just as I also am known." As we work within our Divine Design we see glimpses of God's grace at work in us and in others. These efforts are being combined with others on an ever-growing artistic canvas that dates back millennia. Ultimately this masterpiece will bring the reign of God on earth so that it will be done "on earth as it is in heaven."

In the 1800s Pony Express riders had one assignment — deliver the message safely and quickly. They seized every advantage: The shortest route, the fastest horse; go with the lightest saddle, even the lightest lunchbox. Only the sturdy were hired. Could they handle horses? The heat? Could they outrun robbers and outlast blizzards? The young and the orphans were preferred. Those selected were given $125 a month, a Colt revolver, a lightweight rifle, a bright red shirt, blue trousers and eight hours to cover 80 miles, six days a week. Hard work and high risk, but the message was worth it.[2] Our message is worth it as well. We have a lifesaving message to share, and people are dying to hear it! The role of our Divine Design is to draw attention not to ourselves but to the King and His Kingdom.

You will do it in a way unique to you. Peter was confrontational (Acts 2). Paul used reason (Acts 17). The man healed of blindness used personal testimony (John 9). Matthew threw a party (Luke 5). The woman at the well extended an invitation (John 4). Another woman made clothing and gave it away (Acts 9). All of us relate to others in a way consistent with our God-given design. There is no single right way or best way to spread the good news of God's love, so we must be careful of falling in love with "our way."

Perhaps you heard the story of the frog in the middle of a relocation (there's that frog again!). He had a problem. His home pond was drying up. And if he didn't find water soon, he would do the same. Word reached him of the stream over an adjacent hill. If only he could get there. But the short legs of a frog were not made for long journeys.

Then he came upon an idea. Convincing two birds to carry either end of a stick, he bit the center and held on as they flew. As they headed toward the new water, his jaws clamped tightly. It was quite a sight! Two birds, one stick, and a frog in the middle. Down below, a cow in a pasture saw the trio passing overhead. Impressed, he wondered aloud, "Who came up with that idea?" The frog overheard his question and couldn't resist a prideful reply: "I diiiiiiiiii . . ."

In your excitement over discovering your Divine Design it would be very easy to overestimate your own importance. After all, you are fearfully and wonderfully made (Psalm 139:14). But you were not made for yourself. In our church we emphasize over and over "It's not about me!" It starts with God, ends with God and in the middle of it all is . . . others.

In the movie *Chariots of Fire*, Eric Liddell represented Britain in the 400 meter sprint in the 1924 Olympic Games. Eric, who is a committed Christian, is handed a scrap of paper from a fellow athlete that has I Samuel 2:30 written on it: "He who honors Me, I will honor." He clutches that paper tightly in his fist as he sprints toward the finish line to win his gold medal. As the camera closes in on his straining, sweaty face we hear Eric's now-famous words: "God made me fast, and when I run, I feel His pleasure." Eric had discovered his Kingdom purpose. While there were many things he may have excelled at, there was one that allowed him to feel God's pleasure more than anything else, and that was his running. In the movie we get to see how God uses that unique gift to bring glory to Himself.

What is it that you do that helps you to feel God's pleasure? Chances are, that's where you will be a force for His Kingdom.

This poem sums up the confidence you can have in determining God's will:

> You are who you are for a reason.
> You're part of an intricate plan.
> You're a precious and perfect unique design
> Called God's special woman or man.
>
> You look like you look for a reason.
> Our God made no mistake.
> He knit you together within the womb,
> You're just what He wanted to make.
>
> The parents you had were the ones He chose,
> And no matter how you may feel,
> They were custom-designed with God's plan in mind,
> And they bear the Master's seal.
>
> No, that trauma you faced was not easy.
> And God wept that it hurt you so;
> But it was allowed to shape your heart
> So that into His likeness you'd grow.
>
> You are who you are for a reason,
> You've been formed by the Master's rod.
> You are who you are, beloved,
> Because there is a God![3]

Reflection

1. Complete this sentence inspired by Eric Liddell: "God made me to _____ and when I _____ I feel His pleasure."

2. Most people use their gifts, talents and experience to benefit themselves. Imagine your Divine Design focused on God's purposes. Explain how your life might be different.

3. Since God has communicated His purpose for you through how He has created and called you, what then is your responsibility?

4. Imagine yourself face to face with God in heaven. Your life review is under way and you are about to have a specific discussion about how you used your Divine Design to further God's Kingdom on earth. Based upon your life actions up to this point, will the discussion be animated or disappointing? What could you do now to change that?

5. Read I Corinthians 9:19-23. What do Paul's words have to do with our Divine Design? What part of your design can you best use to influence others for Christ's cause?

CHAPTER 50

A NEW LIFE STORY

*We err greatly . . . in thinking that we will remain who we are at the time
of death. God created us for growth, and surely that growth will continue
into eternity. We are only at the beginning point of becoming who we will be,
the end result of which is unimaginable because none of us can comprehend
eternal life, much less what it means to reach perfection.*[1]
— Tom Paterson

The legacy of your Divine Design will be seen through the effectiveness of your service. We are not just to discover and develop our spiritual
SHAPE, but to deploy it. As I write this, we have members of our congre-
gation who have been deployed to Iraq to serve in the war effort. When
you are deployed, you are put into service. You get out in the field and start
doing something with your abilities. Romans 12:6 (TEV) states, "We are
to use our different gifts in accordance with the grace God's given us . . ."
This maximizes our contribution.

In the final scene of the movie *Mr. Holland's Opus*, Glenn Holland
(played by Richard Dreyfus) has just retired from his job of 30 years, teaching music at a high school in a small American community. Talking with
his closest friend, the school's football coach, Glenn tearfully laments that
he does not think he has made any difference in the decades he has spent
in what he refers to as "this gig." Despite assurances from his friend that he
has made a difference, Mr. Holland sits dejectedly in what had become the
most important place in his life, and in the lives of many of his students
– his music room.

As he is leaving the school with his wife and son, he enters the auditorium and is greeted by hundreds of his former students, who upon hearing
of his retirement, have come to celebrate and thank him for the difference
he has made in each of their lives, and in their development as human
beings. One of them, now governor of the state, softly chides Mr. Holland for entertaining the idea that he had not made a difference. Instead,
she suggests, he has had a profound impact on the lives of everyone in
the auditorium. The development of every one of these people, which had
become his life's labor, had become his true opus, his "real" symphony and
the legacy by which he will be remembered.

All of us are creating a symphony with our life. We use our gifts, skills, personality, experience and passions to compose a musical score that is uniquely ours but bears the mysteriously delightful refrain of the One who made us. Oh, there may be a wrong note or two, or perhaps a measure out of tune, but keep on playing!

Norman Vincent Peale said, "No matter what mistakes you have made – no matter how you messed things up – you can still make a new beginning. The person who fully realizes this suffers less from the shock and pain of failure and sooner gets off to a new beginning."[2]

My wife and I both enjoy gardening and take particular delight in rescuing plants from the local nursery that have been discounted because of their appearance. There are wonderful bargains to be had, especially in mid-summer, when the pictures attached to a particular flower look nothing at all like its faded and wilted glory. But we've discovered the key. We don't look at the full blossoms – their time is past. We look to see how many healthy new buds are starting to form. If there are many, we know that when that plant is brought home, in a matter of weeks we can have it blossoming beautifully!

As we start our new life story, the focus isn't on what has passed or the faded glory of what currently is. No, it is time to focus on the new life – the blossoms that are ready to burst into new beauty. If you will trust the Master Gardener to do your pruning, your life will soon be in full bloom.

Continue to look at the resources you've been given in life to discern clues about how God intends to use you. Your backpack is filled with the equipment you need to get you to your destination. Don't be surprised if your destination is not the same as everyone else's. If your faith in your uniqueness is small, consider this:

> Each of us has the capacity to generate $10^{3,000}$ eggs or sperm
> with unique sets of genes. If we consider $10^{3,000}$ possible eggs
> being generated by an individual woman and the same number
> of sperm being generated by an individual man, the likelihood
> of anyone else with your set of genes, in the past or in the future,
> becomes infinitesimal.[3]

While you are totally unique, don't forget that you have been shaped for a purpose.

Robert Cooper tells the story of his early love of baseball. One day, discouraged, he said to his grandfather, "I'm going to quit the game." His grandfather led him to a small, dusty storage building outside his house. He reached on a high shelf and retrieved a dusty baseball glove, thick-fingered and darkened with age. Robert tells how his grandfather took his handkerchief, gently cleaned off the glove and handed it to him. His grandfather explained that the glove had belonged to his younger brother, Will, who was an early devotee of the game in the early 1900s. Robert was instructed to try it on. As he slid his hand inside, he could feel the distinct impression of another hand. His grandfather explained that the glove had been soaked in leather oil and then wrapped tightly around a baseball at night beside his pillow. Through the innumerable practices and games, the finger pocket of the glove had taken the exact shape of Will's fingers and palm. "You are touching his hand," his grandfather told him. "Will taught many children how to play the game, and when he died, I kept his glove," his grandfather went on, "and when I slide my hand inside I can feel the shape of his hand, a memory of the trace he left on me and everyone around him."[4]

The glove we slip on has been shaped by our Savior. We have a unique imprint and when we place the glove on our hand, the two blend in a wonderful divine partnership. So go on . . .

> To lead by example,
> To love as if you will live forever,
> To work as if you have no need for money,
> Dream as if no one can say no,
> Have fun as if you never have to grow up,
> Sing as if no one is listening,
> Care as if everything depends on your caring,
> And raise a banner where a banner never flew.[5]

You've learned to examine your Divine Design. You've looked at your spiritual SHAPE, your spiritual gifts, your heart, abilities, personality and life experiences. You've examined the opportunities before you and recognized how you must trust God to help you. But everything up to this point is prologue. Your story is only beginning. God wants to partner with you to keep working on your Divine Design. You were created for His glory and purpose. He could have had you placed at any point in history, but

He chose to give you this hour. He did this because now is the time when you can make the greatest difference. Are you ready? It's time to move from your Divine Design into your Divine destiny!

On the surface, I am an average person,
but to my heart I am not an average person.
To my heart, I am a great moment.
The challenge I face is how to dedicate everything
I have inside me to fulfilling this moment.
  – Abraham Heschel

REFLECTION

1. Ask a few of your friends to jot down the two or three things that your life represents for them – things they would desperately miss without your acquaintance. Do their answers reflect what you had thought they would see? Do they match any part of your Divine Design?

2. James Bilkey once observed, "You will never be the person you can be if pressure, tension and discipline are taken out of your life." As you look back, can you see places where your problems were actually aids in developing your Divine Design?

3. How does it make you feel to know that there never was a person exactly like you and there never will be? How does this speak to using your gifts and talents in a way that pleases God and helps others?

4. Write a paragraph describing the kind of life and experiences you hope to have when fully utilizing your Divine Design. Now commit your dream to prayer and ask for God's help.

5. Read John 10:10. What implication does this verse have for you as you follow your Divine Design?

CONCLUSION

If you ended this study thinking you would have all the answers to your questions about your Divine Design, I am sorry to disappoint you. Learning about yourself will be a lifelong process.

It's okay not to have everything completely resolved in your mind. German poet Rainer Maria Rilke wrote in his book *Letters to a Young Poet*:

> Be patient to all that is unsolved in your heart and try to love the questions themselves like locked rooms and like books that are written in a very foreign tongue . . . and the point is, to live everything. Live the questions now. Perhaps you will then gradually, without noticing it, live along some distant day to the answer.[1]

Here's an acrostic that will help you GRASP your Divine Design:

G – Get with God: While a contact with God may be important, a connection with Him is vital. He must be at the center of our lives if we hope to let go of the many things that distract us from our FOCUS.

R – Reach for your Kingdom dream: The deeper your relationship with God, the more you want to cooperate with Him for His purpose. Spend time alone with Him so that you can hear Him clearly.

A – Align with your strengths: You have specific wiring that is critical to your fruitfulness and fulfillment. In this wiring lies a sweet spot – the intersection of the way that you're made and the opportunities you're given – in which you can perform with maximum effectiveness. Make this your focus.

S – Seek support: None of us can go it alone. We need to be a part of a church that understands that we're all called to minister. So we need to serve on a team with complementary gifts and abilities.

P – Practice persistently: We must never give up. Adversity will only strengthen our faith so that we can go farther longer. Our lifetime is to be used serving God and others with our Divine Design.

I leave you these words spoken by Nelson Mandela

Our deepest fear is not that we are inadequate,
our deepest fear is that we are powerful beyond measure.
It is our light, not our darkness that most frightens us.
We ask ourselves, who am I to be brilliant, gorgeous, talented, and
fabulous–actually, who are you not to be?
You are a child of God.
Your playing small doesn't serve the world.
There's nothing enlightened about shrinking so that other people
won't feel insecure around you.
We were born to make manifest the glory of God within us.
It is not just in some of us: It is in everyone,
and as we let our own light shine, we unconsciously
give other people permission to do the same.[2]

A WORD TO PASTORS

Any follower deserves a competent leader. If we are honest we'd have to admit we've often recruited people to serve and then criticized them for not performing well – even though we didn't affirm them, train them, give them adequate feedback or even take the time to prayerfully consider whether they were right for the job.

There's no question that people often have legitimate reasons for their hesitancy to get involved in our churches. One national research initiative on the topic of volunteerism and ministry development indicated that the issue was not a lack of desire but a lack of direction as to what to do that kept people from using their gifts in service. Very often the reasons pointed directly to the poor examples of leaders in the church who were not able to express their God-given strengths on a regular basis because they were trying to do it all.

It is surprising how many leaders have no intentional plan for developing the potential of those they lead. Staff and churches often hold tightly to their roles and don't share their ministry with volunteers. Volunteers interviewed by the researchers did not receive appreciation for their efforts and were not given help in how to discover their God-given strengths. People were not given realistic time frames, not followed up after they volunteered, and did not understand how the use of their gifts was helping to further the overall mission of the church. Often ministry workers receive very limited training and orientation, and there is a lack of appreciation, feedback and support.

Those who lead our churches have the responsibility to provide a system and process whereby people can use their gifts to maximum effect. Within every ministry of the church there should be a means to attract, to attach and to activate those within its circle.

Imagine the thrill of describing a picture to your entire church family of the overarching purpose of their lives and then giving them a canvas on which to paint it.

Let's be sure that our congregations are receiving God's directives and affirmations. The world and the devil beat them up week in and week out, and we must offer God's gracious approval and help. How many of these truths do you emphasize with those you lead?

- I am accepted (Romans 15:7)
- I am loved (Jeremiah 31:3)
- I am free (John 8:32)
- I am forgiven (Isaiah 43:25)
- I am saved (II Timothy 1:9)
- I am victorious (Romans 8:37)
- I am complete (Colossians 2:10)
- I am protected (Psalm 17:8)
- I am chosen (I Thessalonians 1:4)
- I am a masterpiece (Ephesians 2:10)

Once leaders affirm these biblical truths, we have a responsibility to help our people be equipped to serve (Ephesians 4:11). There must be a plan in place to help them discover their Divine Design and a process to care for the people who volunteer to serve others.

Church leaders have a responsibility to those they lead to fulfill certain serving expectations such as:

- Matching volunteers to assignments that are their Divine Design
- Giving them affirmation
- Cultivating an openness to new ideas
- Being willing to see the big picture
- Offering training and using a volunteer's time wisely
- Making sure that the volunteer opportunity includes spiritual development

At BranchCreek Community Church, we used *Discovering Your Divine Design* as the basis for a spiritual growth campaign that seeks to align all our efforts as a church over an eight-week period to help people use their God-given designs in ministry and service.

Anticipation for the study grows through extensive promotion. Each person in the church is asked to read the daily devotional or listen to an audio CD of the book. They are offered a small-group experience, related service activities, original devotional music by our music team, and weekend teachings that coincide with the same topics. Each of the church's ministries aligns with the overarching emphasis. A ministry fair was conducted to assist in placing people into active service using their newly founded discoveries. Ministry leaders were asked to develop ministry descriptions and first-serve opportunities. Consideration was given to serving possibilities in the community, as well. Monthly ministry support meetings were then offered, with oversight from our pastoral staff.

This process has helped our large and growing church stay together and focused. We would be happy to make our materials and experiences available to help your church members focus on their Divine Design.

✻✻✻

"Imagine the thrill of describing a picture to your entire church family of the overarching purpose of their lives and then giving them a canvas on which to paint it. Let's be sure that our congregations are receiving God's directives and affirmations." (Page 109 in *Discovering Your Divine Design*)

Here is a tool for church leaders who want to help their members find the basis for a fulfilling ministry, based on what God is already doing in their lives. Fifty chapters—enough for a year of small group discussions—present practical truths with interesting illustrations and provocative questions for reflection. Distilling dozens of books and decades of life experience, Pastor Bishop has pulled together a rich collection of ideas and exercises. With these, whether reading alone or in the context of a small group, readers can learn to appreciate their God-given uniqueness and find fulfillment within it.

"One national research initiative. . .indicated that the issue was not a lack of desire but a lack of direction as to what to do that kept people from using their gifts in service. Those who lead our churches have the responsibility to provide a system and process whereby people can use their gifts to maximum effect." (Page 109 in *Discovering Your Divine Design*)

This book lays out such a system and process, with inspiration included.

— Carl George, noted church consultant and author of *Nine Keys to Effective Small Group Leadership* and *How to Break Growth Barriers*

ENDNOTES

Chapter 1
1. Robert K. Cooper, *The Other 90%* (New York, NY: Crown Business, 2001), 98.
2. Genesis 1:26, 27.
3. Bob Gass, *Discovering Your Destiny* (Gainesville, FL: Bridge-Logos, 2001), 42.
4. Verses 13-16 (NIV)

Chapter 2
1. *Our Daily Bread* (Grand Rapids, MI: Radio Bible Class Ministries, June 15, 2006).
2. Keith Miller and Bruce Larson, *The Passionate People* (Waco, TX: Word Books, 1979), 14.
3. Erik Reese, *S.H.A.P.E.* (Grand Rapids, MI: Zondervan, 2006), 21.

Chapter 3
1. Søren Kierkegaard, Purity of Heart is to Will One Thing, 140, quoted in Lucado, *Cure for the Common Life* (Nashville, TN: Thomas Nelson, 2005), 18.

Chapter 4
1. Bob Buford, *Game Plan* (Grand Rapids, MI: Zondervan, 1997), 67.
2. Max Lucado, *Cure for the Common Life* (Nashville, TN: Thomas Nelson, 2005), 20.

Chapter 6
1. Rick Warren, *The Purpose Driven Life* (Grand Rapids, MI: Zondervan, 2002), 237.
2. Bruce Bugbee, *What You Do Best in the Body of Christ* (Grand Rapids, MI: Zondervan, 2005), 47-48.

Chapter 7
1. Jane Kise, David Stark, Sandra Hirsh, *Life Keys* (Grand Rapids, MI: Bethany House, 1996), 187.

2. Adapted from Erik Reese, 38-45.

Chapter 8
1. I Corinthians 12:17-21, 24-26.

Chapter 9
1. Warren, 238.
2. Buford, 74-75.
3. Richard Chang, *The Passion Plan* (San Francisco, CA: Jossey-Bass, 2000), xxvii.
4. Aubrey Malphurs, *Maximizing Your Effectiveness* (Grand Rapids, MI: Baker Books, 1995), 33.
5. Romans 1:9, Ephesians 6:6.

Chapter 10
1. Erwin Raphael McManus, *Seizing Your Divine Moment* (Nashville, TN: Thomas Nelson, 1998), 155.
2. Tom Paterson, *Living the Life You Were Meant to Live* (Nashville, TN: Thomas Nelson, 1998), 155.
3. John L. Mason, *You're Born an Original, Don't Die a Copy* (Altamonte Springs, FL: Insight International, 1993), 16.

Chapter 11
1. Mason, 14.
2. Ed Young, *You!* (West Monroe, LA: Howard Publishing House, 2005), 23.
3. Philippians 2:13.

Chapter 12
1. Max Lucado, *Shaped by God* (Wheaton, IL: Tyndale, 1985), 3-4.

Chapter 13
1. Mels Carbonell, *What Makes You Tick* (Blue Ridge, GA: Uniquely You Resources, 1997), 54.
2. Ibid, 64-65.
3. Florence Littauer, *Personality Plus* (Grand Rapids, MI: Fleming H. Revell, 1992), 3.

Chapter 14
1. Anonymous.
2. Arthur F. Miller, Jr., *Why You Can't Be Anything You Want to Be* (Grand Rapids, MI: Zondervan, 1999), 190.
3. Robin Chaddock, *Discovering Your Divine Assignment* (Eugene, OR: Harvest House, 2005), 126.

Chapter 15
1. See I Samuel 17, especially 34-37.

Chapter 16
1. See Genesis 45.
2. Paterson, 44.

Chapter 18
1. Lucado, *Cure for the Common Life*, 35.

Chapter 20
1. *Our Daily Bread* (Grand Rapids, MI: Radio Bible Class Ministries) Dec. 4, 2004.
2. Job 10:8-9, Psalm 119:73, Isaiah 29:16, 64:8.
3. Verses 13-15 (MES).

Chapter 21
1. Radio Bible Class, June 18, 2006.

Chapter 22
1. Walt Kallestad, *Be Your Own Creative Coach* (Grand Rapids, MI: Zondervan, 1998), 14.
2. Paterson, 193-195.
3. Craig Groeschel, *Chazown* (Sisters, OR: Multnomah, 2006), 26.

Chapter 23
1. Leonard Sweet, *The Jesus Prescription for a Healthy Life* (Nashville, TN: Abingdon, 1996), 194.
2. John Ortburg, *The Life You've Always Wanted* (Grand Rapids, MI: Zondervan, 1997), 122.

Chapter 24
1. Hyram W. Smith, *The 10 Natural Laws of Successful Time & Life Management* (New York, NY: Warner Books, 1994), 46.
2. Ibid, 49.
3. Proverbs 4:5-7.
4. Rosamund and Benjamin Zander (Boston, MA: Howard Business School Press, 2000), 65.

Chapter 25
1. Radio Bible Class, June 26.

Chapter 26
1. Chaddock, 11.

Chapter 27
1. Lucado, *Cure for the Common Life*, 132.
2. Reese, 205.
3. Ibid, 135.
4. Ibid, 138.

Chapter 28
1. C. S. Lewis, *Letters to Malcolm Chiefly on Prayer* (San Diego, CA: Harcourt, 1964), 69.

Chapter 29
1. Neva Coyle, *Free to Dream* (Minneapolis, MN: Bethany, 1990), 33.

Chapter 30
1. Kallestad, 123.
2. Gass, 69-70.

Chapter 31
1. Rosamund and Benjamin Zander, *The Art of Possibility* (Boston, MA: Howard Business School Press, 2000), 116-117.
2. Ibid, 117.

Chapter 32
1. Frank R.Tillapaugh, *Unleashing Your Potential* (Ventura, CA: Regal Books, 1988), 82-83.

Chapter 33
1. Luke 16:10.

Chapter 34
1. Reese, 106.
2. Kallestad, 38.
3. Ibid.

Chapter 35
1. Stephen R. Covey, *First Things First* (New York, NY: Fireside, 1994), 103.
2. Buford, 115.
3. Ibid, 119.

Chapter 36
1. Ecclesiastes 11:4 (TLB).

Chapter 37
1. Luke 6:30 (NIV).
2. John Mason, *Imitation Is Limitation* (Bloomington, MN: Bethany, 2004), 86-87.
3. Ephesians 3:20 (TLB).

Chapter 38
1. Chaddock, 15.
2. Lucado, *Cure for the Common Life*, 122.

Chapter 39
1. Laurie Beth Jones, *The Path: Creating Your Mission Statement* (New York: Hyperion, 1996), 68.
2. Groeschel, 188.
3. Bob Briner, *Roaring Lambs* (Grand Rapids, MI: Zondervan, 1993), 18.

Chapter 40
1. Robert C. Roberts, "Just A Little Bit More," *Christianity Today*, April 8, 1996, 30.
2. Kise, Stark, Hirsh, 221.
3. Roberts, 30.

4. Groeschel, 156-157.
5. Zander and Zander, 89-90.

Chapter 42
1. Joe Vitale, *Missing Instruction Manual* (Hoboken, NJ: John Wiley and Sons, 2006), 80.

Chapter 43
1. David Cottrell, *12 Choices That Lead to Your Success* (Dallas, TX: Corner Stone Leadership Institute, 2005), 123.
2. Covey, 200.

Chapter 44
1. McManus, 76-77.

Chapter 45
1. Richard N. Bolles, *How to Find Your Mission in Life* (Berkeley, CA: Ten Speed Press, 2000), 11.

Chapter 46
1. Chang, 14.
2. Lucado, *It's Not About Me*, 39-40.
3. Andy Stanley, *Visioneering* (Sisters, OR: Multnomah Press, 1999), 247.

Chapter 47
1. Joseph Jaworski, *Synchronicity* (San Francisco, CA: Barrett-Koehler Publishers, 1998), 137.
2. Lucado, *Shaped by God*, 112.
3. Source unknown.

Chapter 48
1. I Corinthians 12:4-7.
2. Marcus Buckingham and Curt Coffman, *First, Break All the Rules* (New York, NY: Simon & Schuster, 1999), 168.

Chapter 49
1. Lucado, *Cure for the Common Life*, 51.
2. Lucado, *It's Not About Me*, 89.
3. Warren, 25.

Chapter 50
1. Paterson, 240.
2. Mason, *Imitation Is Limitation*, 98.
3. Lucado, *Cure for the Common Life*, 32.
4. Cooper, 263-264.
5. Ibid, 273.

Conclusion
1. Lucia Capacchione and Peggy Van Pelt, *Putting Your Talent to Work* (Deerfield Beach, FL: Health Communications, Inc. 1996), 206.
2. Zander and Zander, 178.

RESOURCES

Other Books by Dr. S. Craig Bishop

2004

Emerging Faith

This book is the first of Craig's 50-day devotionals designed for both personal and church-wide study. Packed with illustrations and a built-in study guide, this book examines common misconceptions about faith and how to help it grow.

A popular study guide and journal written by chuck faber will help to amplify and enhance your learning.

2005

Faithspace in the Workplace
with Matthew Bishop

Did you get the memo? God is at work!

Faithspace in the Workplace describes a personal God who takes His children beyond the pursuit of wealth, recognition and success into an exciting partnership to pursue His purposes for the world. Learn how to see your vocation from an external point of view and discover the meaning and joy that comes from faith *at work.*

Also available on audio CD

2007

Discovering Your Divine Design Audio Book

Take *Discovering Your Divine Design* with you in the car or use the author's own rendition of the book in your next small group meeting. Cement these important spiritual concepts in your mind by listening to them over and over.

Various other training resources are available on request.

APPENDIX 1: TRANSLATIONS

The translations used throughout this book were purposely varied to provide clarity and to add interest. Verses are not always included in their entirety in the text but can be referenced through the endnote designation.

Contemporary English Version
New York: American Bible Society (1995)

God's Word Translation
Grand Rapids: Word Publishing, Inc. (1995)

The Living Bible
Wheaton, Illinois: Tyndale House Publishers (1979)

The Message
Colorado Springs: NavPress (1993)

New English Version
London, England: Oxford University Press and Cambridge University Press (1961, 1970)

New International Version
Colorado Springs: International Bible Society (1978, 1984)

New King James Version
Nashville, Tennessee: Thomas Nelson (1979, 1980, 1982)

New Living Translation
Wheaton, Illinois: Tyndale House Publishers (1996)

New Revised Standard Version
Grand Rapids: Zondervan (1990)

New Testament in Modern English by J. B. Phillips
New York: McMillan (1958)

Revised Standard Version
New York: Collins (1946)

Today's English Version (also called Good News Translation)
New York: American Bible Society (1992)

Today's New International Version
Grand Rapids: Zondervan (2005)

APPENDIX 2:
CONTACT INFORMATION

Your comments are most welcome.
Your stories feed me.
Please let me know how this book affects your life
or how your church or Bible study is using it for spiritual growth.

You can e-mail me at Craig@BranchCreek.org
or address mail to:
Dr. S. Craig Bishop
100 South Main Street,
Harleysville, Pennsylvania 19438

For additional help or information, feel free to contact:
BranchCreek Community Church
100 South Main Street
Harleysville, Pennsylvania 19438
Phone: 215.256.0100
Fax: 215.256.0580
Web site: www.branchcreek.org
Senior Pastor: S. Craig Bishop, D.Min.

For pastors and church leaders: An eight-week Sunday morning teaching series to accompany this book was conducted at BranchCreek Community Church in the fall of 2007. Supplemental materials from the series are available by contacting the church at the above address.